The
Aspen
Institute

AMERICA AND THE MUSLIM MIDDLE EAST: MEMOS TO A PRESIDENT

An Aspen Policy Book

Edited by

Philip D. Zelikow

and

Robert B. Zoellick

For additional copies of this report, please contact:
The Aspen Institute
Publications Office
109 Houghton Lab Lane
PO Box 222
Queenstown, MD 21658
Telephone: (410) 820-5326
Fax: (410) 827-9174
E-mail: publications@aspeninst.org

For all other inquiries, please contact:
The Aspen Institute
Aspen Strategy Group
1333 New Hampshire Avenue, NW
Suite 1070
Washington, DC 20036
Telephone: (202) 736-5800
Fax: (202) 467-0790

ISBN: 0-89843-239-1
98-015

Table of Contents

Introduction

I magine that a president of the United States gathers respected experts to join his advisers in the wooded hills of Maryland, at the presidential retreat of Camp David, for a broad discussion of a topic. Imagine further that the president chooses the topic of "America and the Muslim Middle East." Why? The topic is one that regularly commands his daily attention, but always in bits of news, the day's cables or correspondence, or a particular meeting. The president wants to approach the topic in more depth and gain a broader perspective. In this the president is no different from any student, any citizen, diverted by headlines or individual stories, who wants to take more time—but not a great deal of time—to comprehend the issues better. What he or she needs is not just a compendium of longer opinion pieces or pointed advocacy. Instead the president needs background and context, oriented to the operational policy challenges of the government.

What could be helpful for busy presidents might, we thought, be of interest to busy citizens. So this book presents our distillation of a White House policy seminar that never happened. We use the real experts and former top policymakers brought together in August 1997 by the Aspen Strategy Group, a program of The Aspen Institute. The discussions were chaired by Sam Nunn and Kenneth Dam. At a real Camp David meeting, the papers might be somewhat shorter and more focused on the events of the coming week or month; the discussions would be briefer; there probably would have been few or no foreign guests; and the paper record would have been less complete. Nevertheless we think this book captures much of the quality, and value, of the genuine article.

The book is organized around four "sessions," each structured around a different set of memos and guest experts. Each session begins with a brief staff outline of the questions the staff thinks are raised and ought to be discussed. The memos are presented next, each reflecting the author's particular perspective on the topic assigned. Third is a staff summary of points that, to them, seemed to emerge from the discussion. Please note: as at a real Camp David dialogue, all the Aspen Strategy Group participants want to speak freely; therefore they are promised that no one will be quoted by name. In fact, confronted with our summaries of the discussion, several participants would say (or did say) either that they disagreed with the views being summarized, that they remained silent without joining in the reported view, or that they find their opinions inadequately captured by such meager summaries. All true. So we can only echo the excuse that has been offered by note takers throughout recorded history: We did our best. These are our impressions of the discussion, and ours alone. The views noted here do not express the opinions or conclusions of others who participated.

Our sessions begin with a general overview of what a president needs to understand about the Muslim world. Then we move from large themes to specific exemplars, choosing three countries and regional environments: Saudi Arabia, Iran, and Turkey. Incidentally, the papers have been updated to reflect developments as of March 1998.

We would like to thank the many people who have contributed to and assisted with publishing this report. First, we thank the Aspen Strategy Group Co-Chairmen, Kenneth Dam and Sam Nunn, who lend their leadership and moderation skills to the program. We are grateful to the writers, who all contributed outstanding papers to our meeting and to this volume, and who were an integral part of the Group's discussions. We thank the Aspen Strategy Group members for their continued dedication to the program and its goals.

We are especially grateful to the Carnegie Corporation of New York and the John D. and Catherine T. MacArthur Foundation for the generous support they have provided the Aspen Strategy Group over the years, and for their support of this meeting and publication in particular.

Philip Zelikow
Robert B. Zoellick

Discussants and Guest Experts

ASPEN STRATEGY GROUP
"AMERICA AND THE MUSLIM MIDDLE EAST"
AUGUST 16-21, 1997

Shaul Bakhash, professor of history at George Mason University

Marouf Bakhit-Nader, major general in the Jordanian army, now serving at Mutah University

HRH Bandar bin Sultan, ambassador to the United States of the Kingdom of Saudi Arabia

Richard Burt, chairman of IEP Advisors, Inc., former U.S. ambassador to Germany, arms control negotiator, and assistant secretary of state

Richard Cooper, professor of economics at Harvard University, former chair of the U.S. National Intelligence Council, and former undersecretary of state

Kenneth Dam, professor of law at University of Chicago and former deputy secretary of state

Edward Djerejian, director of the Baker Institute at Rice University, former U.S. ambassador to Syria, and former assistant secretary of state

Thomas Donilon, attorney, former assistant secretary of state, and former White House official

Haleh Esfandiari, professor of government at George Mason University

Abdulaziz H. Al Fahad, attorney in Riyadh, Saudi Arabia

Leslie Gelb, president of the Council on Foreign Relations, former columnist and correspondent with the *New York Times,* and former assistant secretary of state

Bryan Hehir, professor of religion and society at Harvard University and counselor to Catholic Relief Services

Arnold Horelick, vice president for Russian and Eurasian affairs at the Carnegie Endowment for International Peace, and former analyst at the RAND Corporation

Robert Hormats, investment banker, former assistant secretary of state, and former National Security Council official

Karen Elliott House, publishing executive and foreign correspondent with the *Wall Street Journal*

Bobby Inman, retired admiral, former chairman of the Federal Reserve Bank of Dallas, and former senior defense and intelligence official

Arnold Kanter, senior analyst for the Forum for International Policy and the RAND Corporation, former undersecretary of state, and former National Security Council official

Lawrence Korb, senior analyst for the Brookings Institution and former assistant secretary of defense

Martin Kramer, professor and director of Dayan Center at Tel Aviv University

Bernard Lewis, professor of Near Eastern studies emeritus at Princeton University

Jan Lodal, principal deputy undersecretary of defense and former corporate CEO

Heath Lowry, professor of Ottoman and Modern Turkish studies at Princeton University

Jessica Mathews, president of the Carnegie Endowment for International Peace and former National Security Council official

Judith Miller, senior writer with the *New York Times*

Janne Nolan, senior analyst for the Brookings Institution and member of the Pentagon's Defense Policy Board

Sam Nunn, attorney and former U.S. senator from Georgia

Joseph Nye, Jr., dean of the Kennedy School at Harvard University, former assistant secretary of defense, and former chair of the U.S. National Intelligence Council

Olivier Roy, senior researcher at the Centre National de la Recherche Scientifique in Paris and former OSCE special envoy to Tajikistan

Robert Satloff, executive director of the Washington Institute for Near East Policy

Daniel Schorr, senior news analyst with National Public Radio and former correspondent for Cable Network News and CBS News

Brent Scowcroft, director of the Forum for International Policy and former national security adviser to Presidents Bush and Ford

Koji Watanabe, senior fellow at the Japan Center for International Exchange, former Japanese ambassador to Saudi Arabia, Russia, and Italy, and former deputy minister of the foreign ministry

William Webster, attorney, former director of the CIA and of the FBI, and former federal judge

Philip Zelikow, professor at Harvard University and former White House official and diplomat

Robert Zoellick, professor at the U.S. Naval Academy, former executive vice president at Fannie Mae, and former deputy White House chief of staff and undersecretary of state

Observers at the discussions included **Kennette Benedict** *of the John D. and Catherine T. MacArthur Foundation and* **David Robinson** *and* **Astrid Tuminez** *of the Carnegie Corporation of New York.*

THE MUSLIM WORLD

MEMORANDUM FOR THE PRESIDENT

From: Your Staff

Subject: Questions for Discussion on the Muslim World

1. How is the Muslim world adapting to modernity and globalization?

   - Economic development (example of Muslim Middle East compared with Muslim Southeast Asia)

   - Political development: What is the key variable—Islam, the nation, or the state?

2. How do Muslim states relate to one another?

3. Around the world, is Islamic extremism surging or ebbing? To what extent will the United States be its target?

4. Does the United States need a transnational policy toward "Islam"?

5. How should such a policy regard domestic governance in Muslim states?

   A. With indifference? (Illustration: Should the United States base its policy toward Egypt solely on its international behavior?)

   B. With limited declarations of preference? (Illustration: Should the United States announce that Egypt should do more to uphold human rights, gender equality, or the rule of law? Be more democratic?)

   C. Differentiating "rogue" or "backlash" states because of their domestic behavior? (Illustration: Should the United States penalize Egypt if it crushes domestic dissent?)

   D. With broader intervention/pressure/engagement with opposition? (Illustration: Should the United States press Egypt's president Hosni Mubarak to share power with the Muslim Brotherhood? Open our own diplomatic dialogue with the Brotherhood?)

MEMORANDUM FOR THE PRESIDENT

From: Bernard Lewis

Subject: What You Should Know about Islam

It is difficult to generalize about Islam. To begin with, the word itself is commonly used with two related but distinct meanings, as the equivalents both of Christianity and of Christendom. In the one sense, it denotes a religion, a system of belief and worship; in the other, the civilization that grew up and flourished under the aegis of that religion. The late Marshall Hodgson of Chicago University, a leading authority on Islamic history, proposed the term "Islamdom" in the latter sense. Understandably, but unfortunately, this term did not pass into common usage. I shall, however, use it in this paper to avoid confusion.

Islamdom at the present time comprises more than a billion people. The Organization of the Islamic Conference (OIC) numbers 54 member states, plus five with observer status. Two of these states, Albania and Bosnia-Herzegovina, are in Europe; one, Surinam, is in the Western Hemisphere. The rest are in Asia and Africa and with few exceptions gained their independence in the last half century from the West European and, more recently, the Soviet empires. Most of them are overwhelmingly Muslim in population, though a few were admitted on the strength of Muslim minorities. Apart from these states, there are also significant Muslim minorities in other countries—some of them akin to the majority, as in India, some of them ethnically as well as religiously different, like the Chechens and Tatars of the Russian Federation. Some countries, like China, have Muslim minorities of both kinds.

But this has now changed with the migration of millions of Muslims, principally from North Africa, the Middle East and South Asia, into Western Europe and North America. These are adding a new dimension to Islamdom.

In space, Islamdom as a majority culture extends from Morocco to Indonesia, from Kazakhstan to Senegal. In time it goes back more than 14 centuries, to the advent and mission of the Prophet Mohammed in the seventh century and the creation of the Islamic community and state. In its prime, in the period which Western historians call the Middle Ages, Islamdom was the leading civilization in the world, marked as such by its great and powerful kingdoms, its rich and varied industry and commerce, its original and creative sciences and letters.

Islamdom has been termed "the intermediate civilization"—a name that well describes its position both in time and in space. In time, its greatest age lay between the decline of Greco-Roman civilization and the birth of the modern West; in space it lies between the civilizations of Europe and the Americas to the west and of India, China, and Japan to the east. During the past three centuries, the Islamic world has lost its dominance and its leadership and has fallen behind both the modern West and the rapidly modernizing Orient. This widening gap poses increasingly acute problems, for which the rulers, thinkers, and rebels of Islamdom have not yet found answers.

Islam as a religion clearly is not intermediate and is in every respect far closer to the Judeo-Christian tradition than to any of the great religions of Asia such as Hinduism, Buddhism, or Confucianism. The affinities of Judaism and Christianity are well-known and need no description. Judaism and Islam share the belief in a divine law that regulates all aspects of human activity including even food and drink. Christianity and Islam share a common triumphalism without counterpart in any other religion. Compared with the remoter religions of the East, all three Middle Eastern religions, Judaism, Christianity and Islam, are closely related and indeed appear as variants of the same religious tradition.

The great resemblance between Islam and Christianity and the long interaction and many mutual influences between the two have sometimes led observers to overlook the significant differences. The Qur'an, it is said, is the Muslim Bible; the mosque is the Muslim church; the mullahs are the Muslim clergy. All three statements are true, yet all three are seriously misleading. The Old and New Testament each consist of a collection of different books, extending over a long period of time and seen by the believers as embodying divine revelation. The Qur'an, for Muslims, is a single book promulgated by one man, the

Prophet Mohammed, and is itself divine and eternal. The doctrine of the literal divinity and inerrancy of scripture which distinguishes fundamentalist Protestants from other Christian churches is as an article of faith for all Muslims. The term fundamentalist, as used to designate certain Muslim groups, refers to quite different issues.

The mosque indeed is the Muslim church in the sense of a place of communal worship. But one cannot speak of "the Mosque" as one speaks of "the Church"—of an institution with its own hierarchy and laws, in contrast to the state. The mullahs may be described as a clergy in the sociological sense, in that they are professional men of religion, accredited as such by training and certification. But there is no priesthood in Islam—no priestly mediation between God and the believer, no ordination, no sacraments, no rituals that only an ordained clergy can perform. In the past, one would have added that there are no councils or synods, no bishops to define and inquisitors to enforce orthodoxy. This is no longer entirely true.

It is in the realm of politics—domestic, regional and international alike—that we see the most striking differences between Islamdom and the rest of the world. The heads of state or ministers of foreign affairs of the Scandinavian countries and the United Kingdom do not, from time to time, foregather in Protestant summit conferences, nor has it been the practice of the rulers of Greece, Yugoslavia, Bulgaria, and the Soviet Union, temporarily forgetting their political and ideological differences, to hold regular meetings on the basis of their current or previous adherence to the Orthodox Church. Similarly, the Buddhist states of East and Southeast Asia do not constitute a Buddhist bloc at the United Nations, nor for that matter in any other of their political activities. The very idea of such a grouping, based on religion, in the modern world may seem anachronistic and even absurd. It is neither anachronistic nor absurd in relation to Islam. Throughout the tensions of the Cold War and after, more than 50 Muslim governments, including monarchies and republics, conservatives and radicals, practitioners of capitalism and socialism, supporters of the Western bloc, the Eastern bloc, and a whole spectrum of shades of neutrality, built up an elaborate apparatus of international consultation and, on many issues, cooperation.

There were and are important limits to the effectiveness of the OIC as a factor in international politics. The Soviet invasion of Afghanistan in 1979, a flagrant act of aggression against a sovereign Muslim nation, evoked no serious protest. The influence of Soviet protégés among the members of the Organization was sufficient to prevent that. More recently, the Organization has failed to concern itself with the devastating civil wars in such member states as Sudan and Somalia. Nor has its record in regional matters has been impressive. Between 1980 and 1988, two Islamic countries, Iraq and Iran, fought a devastating war, with casualties which far exceeded all the Arab-Israeli wars put together. The OIC did nothing either to prevent or to end this war. In general, the OIC, unlike the Organization of American States and the Organization of African Unity, does not look into human rights and other domestic problems of member states. The OIC should not, however, be discounted. Its cultural and social activities are important and are growing, and the machinery which it provides for regular consultation between member states may increase in importance as the Cold War and its disruptive effects recede into the past.

Turning from international and regional to domestic politics, the difference between Islamdom and the rest of the world, though less striking, is still substantial. In some of the countries that practice multiparty democracy there are political parties with religious designations—Christian in the West, Buddhist in the Orient. But there are relatively few of these parties and still fewer that play a major role. Even with these, religious themes are of minor importance in their programs and their appeals to the electorate.

In many, indeed in most Islamic countries, religion remains a major political factor—far more indeed in domestic than in international or even in regional affairs.

Why this difference? One answer is obvious: most Muslim countries are still profoundly Muslim, in a way and in a sense that most Christian countries are no longer Christian. Admittedly, in many of these countries, Christian beliefs and the clergy who uphold them are still a powerful force, and although their role is not what it was in past centuries, it is by no means insignificant. But in no Christian country at the present time can religious leaders count on the degree of belief and participation that remains normal in the Muslim lands. In few, if any, Christian countries do Christian sanctities enjoy the immunity from critical comment or discussion that is accepted as normal even in ostensibly secular and democratic Muslim societies. Indeed, this privileged immunity has been extended, de facto, to Western countries where Muslim communities are now established and where Muslim beliefs and practices are accorded a level of immunity that neither the Christian majorities nor the Jewish minorities can command. Most important, with very few exceptions, the Christian clergy do not exercise or even claim the kind of public authority that is still normal and accepted in most Muslim countries.

The higher level of religious faith and practice among Muslims as compared with followers of other religions is part of the explanation of the unique Muslim attitude to politics; it is not the whole explanation, since the same attitude may be found in individuals and even in whole groups whose commitment to religious faith and practice is at best perfunctory. Islam is not only a matter of faith and practice; it is also an identity and a loyalty—for many, an identity and a loyalty others. Americans think of their country as one nation, subdivided into many religions, and this approach is now becoming more widespread in the Western, democratic world. For most Muslims, Islam is a single world community, subdivided into many nations.

On the surface, the importation of the Western notion of nationalism changed all this and led to the creation of a series of modern nation-states, extending across the Islamic world from Morocco to Indonesia. But all is not as it appears on the surface. Two examples may suffice. In 1923, after the last Greco-Turkish war, the two governments agreed to solve their minority problems by an exchange of populations— Greeks were sent from Turkey to Greece, Turks were sent from Greece to Turkey. At least, that is how the history books usually tell the story. The facts are somewhat different. The protocol which the two governments signed in Lausanne in 1923 embodying the exchange agreement does not speak of "Greeks" and "Turks." It defines the persons to be exchanged as "Turkish subjects of the Greek Orthodox

religion residing in Turkey" and "Greek subjects of the Muslim religion residing in Greece." The protocol thus recognizes only two types
of identity, the one defined by being the subject of a state, the other by
being an adherent of a religion. It makes no reference to either ethnic
or linguistic nationality. The accuracy of this document in expressing
the intentions of the signatories was confirmed by the actual exchange.
Most of the so-called Greeks from the Anatolian Turkish province of
Karaman spoke Turkish as their mother tongue, but wrote it in the
Greek script and worshipped in Orthodox churches. Most of the so-
called Turks from Greece knew little or no Turkish but commonly
spoke Greek and wrote it in the Turco-Arabic script. A Western observer, accustomed to a Western system of classification, might well have
concluded that what the governments of Greece and Turkey agreed and
accomplished was not an exchange and repatriation of Greek and
Turkish national minorities but rather a double deportation into exile—
of Muslim Greeks to Turkey, of Christian Turks to Greece. To this day,
Greece and Turkey, both Westernizing democracies, one a member, the
other a candidate for membership of the European Union, have a line
for religion on their state-issued identity documents.

My second example is Egypt. There can be few, if any, nations with a
better claim to nationhood—a country sharply defined by both history
and geography, with a continuous history of civilization going back for
more than 5,000 years. But Egyptians have several identities, and for
most of the last 14 centuries, that is, since Egypt became part of the
Arab-Islamic world, the Egyptian identity has rarely been the predominant one, yielding pride of place to the cultural and linguistic identity
of Arabism and above all to the religious identity of Islam. Egypt as a
nation is one of the oldest in the world. Egypt as a nation-state is a
modern creation, and still faces many challenges at home. At the present time, the strongest of these challenges in Egypt as in some other
Muslim countries comes from radical Islamic groups, the kind now
commonly if misleadingly described as "fundamentalist."

The roots of the Islamic relationship between politics and religion and
its difference from those of Judaism and Christianity can be seen in the
narratives of events which constitute the sacred and scriptural history

of all three religions. Moses led his people out of the house of bondage and through the wilderness, but was not permitted to enter the Promised Land. Christ was crucified, and during the early formative centuries the Christians and their church survived as a persecuted minority under pagan rule, until, with the conversion of Constantine, they captured the Roman state and began the long and still continuing debate between church and state in Christendom. Mohammed was his own Constantine. During his lifetime he became a head of state, exercising the normal functions of sovereignty. That is to say, he promulgated laws and dispensed justice, he raised taxes, commanded armies, made war and peace. From the lifetime of its founder, and therefore in its sacred scriptures, Islam is associated in the minds and memories of Muslims with the exercise of political and military power. Mohammed was statesman, judge, and general as well as Prophet. Church and state could not be separated where they did not exist as different institutions or even as different concepts. Classical Islam recognized a distinction between things of this world and things of the next, between pious and worldly considerations. It did not recognize a separate institution, with a hierarchy and laws of its own, to regulate religious matters. In pagan Rome, Caesar was god. In Christendom, Christians were instructed to "render unto Caesar the things which are Caesar's and unto God the things which are God's." In Islam, God is Caesar, and the same divinely revealed law regulates every aspect of a Muslim's life. The state is God's state, the army is God's army, and the enemy is of course God's enemy. In modern times there have been many changes, mainly under Western influences, and institutions and professions have developed which bear a suspicious resemblance to the churches and clerics of Christendom. But these represent a departure from classical Islam, not a return to it.

Does this mean that Islam is a theocracy? In the sense that God is seen as the supreme sovereign, yes indeed. In the sense of government by a priesthood, most definitely not. The emergence of a priestly hierarchy and its assumption of ultimate authority in the state is a modern innovation and is a unique contribution of Khomeini to Islamic thought and practice.

This does not mean that the Islamic revolution in Iran was either unimportant or ineffectual. Like the French and Russian revolutions which it in many ways resembles, it had a tremendous impact, not only at home and among its own people, but among all the countries and peoples with whom it shared a common universe of discourse. Like the French and Russian revolutions in their days, it aroused tremendous hope and enthusiasm. Like these revolutions, it has suffered its Terror and its War of Intervention; like them, it has its Jacobins and its Bolsheviks, determined to crush any sign of pragmatism or moderation. And like these earlier revolutions and more particularly the Russian, it has its own network of agents and emissaries striving in various ways to further the cause of the revolution or at least of the regime that is seen to embody it.

The word *revolution* has been much misused in the modern Middle East, being applied to, or claimed for, many events which would more appropriately designated by the French coup d'état, the German putsch, or the Spanish pronunciamiento. The political experience of the English-speaking peoples provides no equivalent term. What happened in Iran was none of these, but was in its origins an authentic revolutionary movement of change. Like its predecessors, it has in many ways gone badly wrong, leading to tyranny at home, terror and aggression abroad. Unlike revolutionary France and Russia, revolutionary Islam—for the time being at least—lacks the means, the resources, and the skills to become a major world power and threat. The threat that it does offer is primarily, and overwhelmingly, to the Muslims and to Islam itself.

The revolutionary wave in Islam has several components. One of them is a sense of humiliation; the feeling of a community of people accustomed to regard themselves as the sole custodians of God's truth, commanded by Him to bring it to the infidels; who suddenly find themselves dominated by the same infidels, and even when no longer dominated, still profoundly affected in ways that change their way of life, moving them from true Islamic to other paths. To humiliation is added frustration as the various remedies, most of them imported from the West, were tried and one after another failed.

After humiliation and frustration came a third component, necessary for the resurgence: a new confidence and sense of pride that came with the oil crisis of 1973 and the sense of power which this suddenly gave to people who had become accustomed to being kicked around by almost everybody.

In a time of intensifying strains, of faltering ideologies, jaded loyalties, and crumbling institutions, an ideology expressed in Islamic terms offered several advantages: an emotionally familiar basis of group identity, solidarity, and exclusion; an acceptable basis of legitimacy and authority; an immediately intelligible formulation of principles for both a critique of the present and a program for the future. By means of these, Islam could provide the most effective symbols and slogans for mobilization, whether for or against a cause or a regime. Islamic movements also have another immense advantage as contrasted with all their competitors. In the mosques they dispose of a network of association and communication that even the most dictatorial of governments cannot entirely control. Indeed, ruthless dictatorships help them by eliminating competing oppositions.

Radical Islamism, to which it has become customary to give the name Islamic fundamentalism, is not a single homogeneous movement. There are many different types of Islamic fundamentalism in different countries or even sometimes within a single country. Some are state-sponsored—promulgated, used, and promoted by one or another Muslim government for its own purposes; some are genuine popular movements from below. Among state-sponsored Islamic movements, there are several kinds, both radical and conservative, both subversive and preemptive. Conservative and preemptive movements have been started at various times by governments in power, seeking to protect themselves from the revolutionary wave. Such are the movements sponsored by the Egyptians, the Pakistanis and notably the Saudis. The other kind, far more important, comes from below, with an authentic popular base. The first of these to seize power and the most successful in exercising it is the movement known as the Islamic revolution in Iran. Radical Islamic regimes now rule in the Sudan and in much of Afghanistan, and Islamic movements offer major threats in other countries, notably Algeria and Egypt.

The Muslim fundamentalists, unlike the Protestant groups whose name was transferred to them, do not differ from the mainstream on questions of theology and the interpretation of scripture. Their critique is, in the broadest sense, societal. The Islamic world, in their view, has taken a wrong turn. Its rulers call themselves Muslims and make a pretense of Islam, but they are in fact apostates who have abrogated the Holy Law and adopted foreign and infidel laws and customs. The only solution is a return to the authentic Muslim way of life, and for this the removal of the apostate governments is an essential first step. Fundamentalists are anti-Western in the sense that they regard the West as the source of the evil which is corroding Muslim society, but their primary attack is directed against their own rulers and leaders. The murderers of Sadat and their spokesmen made it clear that, for them, the opening to the United States and the peace with Israel were objectionable, but were in themselves merely symptoms of a deeper evil to be remedied by an inner cleansing. In Egypt they murdered the ruler; in Iran they destroyed the regime and created their own—or so it seemed at the time.

The rise of militant fundamentalism has also had an impact (how great it is difficult to say) on the Muslim minorities in Western Europe and North America. These represent a new phenomenon in Muslim history. Classical Muslim jurists and theologians (in Islam, the two are branches of the same profession) devote a good deal of attention to the question of minorities, but most of their discussion relates to the position of non-Muslim minorities under Muslim rule and the extent and conditions of tolerance to be accorded to them. The position of Muslims under a non-Muslim government in contrast receives very little attention. In classical times it was considered principally in relation to two cases: "the infidel in the land of the infidels" who becomes a Muslim, and Muslims who have the misfortune to be conquered by a non-Muslim power. The classical authorities differed on what was to be done. According to one—the predominant—view, Muslims could not and should not live under non-Muslim rule. If such a situation arose, whether by conversion or by conquest, it was the duty of Muslims to leave their homes and go to a Muslim country, even if this involved a mass exodus. According to the other, more lenient view,

Muslims might remain in their homes under non-Muslim rule, provided that the non-Muslim rulers allowed them the free exercise of their religion. The question first arose during the Reconquest in Spain and Portugal and the Crusades in the Levant, and great numbers of Muslims did indeed voluntarily leave their homes for Muslim lands. The expansion of the great European empires into much of the Muslim world made solution by migration impossible and created a new situation for which the theologians and jurists of Islam were able to find appropriate answers. With the exception of the state-imposed atheism of the Soviet Union, the imperial powers were, for good reasons of imperial policy, tolerant in religious matters.

The voluntary migration of great numbers of Muslims from Islamic to Christian lands created an entirely new situation, one that the classical jurists and theologians never envisaged. The situation of these minorities therefore raises issues for which classical teachings provide no clear or obvious answers. Much of the difficulty arises from the fact that Islam is not just a different religion; it represents a different conception of what religion means and defines, closer in many ways to old-fashioned Rabbinic Judaism than to Christianity. Under Islamic rule from the time of the Prophet until the last Muslim empire, that of the Ottomans, Christian and Jewish subjects of the Muslim state enjoyed the degree and form of tolerance prescribed by Islamic law. That is to say, they were subject to certain fiscal and political disabilities, but were allowed the free exercise of their religion and—from a Muslim point of view more important—were allowed to practice and enforce their own laws of personal status in such matters as marriage, divorce, and inheritance, and to maintain and control their own educational institutions. In the British and French empires from which most of the new migrants came, the imperial governments allowed the Muslims and other religious communities the same kind of communal autonomy. To many Muslim newcomers, it seemed not unreasonable to expect similar treatment in their new homes abroad. In fact they received far more, and far less, than they expected; far more personal freedom, but far less communal autonomy. Not only were Muslim laws not recognized by the state; on some matters, as for example the position of women, they could even come into conflict with the laws of the state. It will take some time to resolve the resulting dilemmas, but when solutions are found, they may be of value in the lands of Islam as well as among Muslims in the West.

In view of the present situation, both in the Islamic lands and among minorities, two important facts need to be stressed: first, that most Muslims are not fundamentalists, and second, that most fundamentalists are not terrorists. These facts, when stated, are self-evident, but both need to be restated because they are often forgotten. Both fundamentalists and terrorists have an obvious interest in blurring these distinctions. Both are unintentionally abetted by the media, which naturally speak only of dramatic events and say little or nothing about the vast mass of ordinary decent Muslims going peacefully about their business. But it must be added that the distinctions between Islam and fundamentalism, and between fundamentalism and terrorism, are also blurred by the reluctance of some religious dignitaries and more political leaders to condemn terrorist acts in unambiguous terms. This reluctance has done great harm to the image of Islam among non-Muslim peoples. Another difficulty is that while self-styled Islamic terrorists constitute an infinitesimal minority among Muslims, they provide a large proportion of reported acts of terrorism.

Peaceful, decent Muslims—that is, the overwhelming majority—are understandably distressed and justifiably angry when the name of their religion becomes identified in the West and in other non-Muslim societies with terrorism and with reckless, random murder. Why is it, they ask, that the media never speak of Irish or Basque or South American terrorists as "Christian terrorists" as they commonly speak of Arabs and Iranians as "Muslim terrorists?" The complaint is valid but is often misdirected. Irish and Basque terrorists, though of Christian background, do not present themselves as fighting a holy war for their faith against its enemies. When terrorists in or from Muslim countries define their objectives in national terms—Palestinian, Kurdish or other—the media describe them accordingly. When they proclaim a holy war for Islam, the media inevitably describe them in the terms in which they describe themselves. The anger of Muslims at the common use of the term "Islamic terrorism" is natural, but their complaints should be addressed to those who make the news, not to those who report it.

The key question that occupies Western policymakers at the present time may be stated simply: Is Islam, whether fundamentalist or other, a threat to the West? To this simple question, various simple answers have been given and, as is the way of simple answers, they are mostly misleading. According to one school of thought, after the demise of the Soviet Union and the Communist movement, Islam and Islamic fundamentalism have replaced them as the major threat to the West and the Western way of life. According to another school of thought, Muslims, including radical fundamentalists, are basically decent, peace-loving, pious people, some of whom have been driven beyond endurance by all the dreadful things that we of the West have done to them. We choose to see them as enemies because we have a psychological need of an enemy to replace the defunct Soviet Union.

Both views contain elements of truth; both are dangerously wrong. Islam as such is not an enemy of the West and there are growing number of Muslims, both there and here, who desire nothing better than a closer and more friendly relationship with the West and the development of democratic institutions in their own countries. But a significant number of Muslims, those whom we call fundamentalists, are hostile and dangerous, not because we need an enemy but because they do. Khomeini and his successors made this clear when they defined the United States as "the Great Satan." Satan, for Muslims as for Christians, is not a conqueror or an exploiter; he is a tempter, most dangerous when he smiles. In calling the United States "the Great Satan" fundamentalists do not mean American power, which they mostly despise; they mean American popular culture, which holds an enormous appeal for young Muslims. For the fundamentalists, it is precisely this American popular culture that is the greatest force for evil in the world today. America's freedom is seen as license and depravity; its wealth as corruption, its popular entertainment as a call to sin and crime. The accusation does not lack plausibility.

The seizure of the American hostages in Tehran in 1979 was undertaken not because relations were deteriorating, but because they were improving. The seizure was decided when meetings were held in Algiers between American representatives and those of the relatively moderate prime minister of Iran. Confronted with the danger of a rapprochement, the radical revolutionaries decided on a complete break. The seizure of the hostages was a successful device to accomplish this end.

Since then, there have been some changes of perception and of tactics among Muslims. Some still see the West in general and its present leader the United States as the ancient and irreconcilable enemy of Islam, the one serious obstacle to the restoration of God's faith and law at home and their ultimate universal triumph. For these there is no way but war to the death, in fulfillment of what they see as the commandments of their faith. There are others who, while remaining committed Muslims and well aware of the flaws of modern Western society, nevertheless also see its merits—its inquiring spirit that produced modern science and technology, its concern for freedom that created modern democratic government. These, while retaining their own beliefs and their own culture, seek to join us in reaching toward a freer and better world. There are some again who, while seeing the West as their ultimate enemy and as the source of all evil, are nevertheless aware of its power, and seek some temporary accommodation in order better to prepare for the final struggle. We would be wise not to confuse the second and the third.

MEMORANDUM FOR THE PRESIDENT

From: Martin Kramer

Subject: What You Should Know about Muslim Politics and Society

What should American leaders know about Muslim politics and society? Precisely what most of academe, many denizens of the think tanks, and even some government officials refuse to acknowledge. The simple axiom is simply stated: in the Muslim world, the state is still stronger than society. Bear this in mind, and you cannot go too far wrong.

On the face of it, this appears obvious. If you are an American leader, you can only be struck by longevity of rulers in Muslim lands, especially if it is translated into presidential time. Jordan's King Hussein ascended the throne the year of Dwight Eisenhower's first inauguration; King Hassan II of Morocco, the year of John Kennedy's inauguration. And it is not just the kings who linger. Muammar el-Qaddafi seized power in Libya the year Richard Nixon was inaugurated, Hafez al-Assad effectively took control of Syria the same year. Hosni Mubarak succeeded to the presidency of Egypt the year Ronald Reagan was first inaugurated.

Surely, this is a part of the world where change is slow in coming. But bearing this in mind is not always easy because of the chorus of voices proclaiming otherwise. Authoritarian, personalized, ideological rule is destined to collapse, the political scientists tell us. It did so spectacularly in Eastern Europe and Russia, gradually in Latin America. At the time, journalists rushed off to cover the incredible stories, academics packed their bags and set out to advise the new regimes on the transition to democracy. It was just a matter of time, said experts on the Muslim world, and tired regimes would also implode in the Muslim lands of Asia and Africa. And didn't a precedent for this already exist in the Middle East? Hadn't the Shah collapsed spectacularly? Iran's revolution became the prism through which an entire generation of observers looked at regime and opposition.

The 1990s, many believed, would bring a second Islamist state into being, this time in an Arab country. Algeria was destined to be the first, claimed some analysts. And when the Algerian regime aborted the elections that nearly brought the Islamists to power in 1991, the same analysts called the coup a futile attempt to stem a rising tide. A leading journalist, writing in *Foreign Affairs* in 1992, assured readers that the Algerian coup was "in many ways like the abortive Moscow putsch in 1991; although the process may take longer, it will fail for similar reasons."[1]

One year passed, then two, then the better part of the decade—and the edifice of the Algerian state still stood. The Algerian regime, it became clear, had much firmer foundations than the Moscow putschists. It is still in power today.

Yet the believers in an irresistible Islamism did not relent. In 1993, an American ambassador to an Arab country offered this apocalyptic prognosis:

> I predict, regretfully, that the region is fated to witness a wave of Islamist revolutions, successful or failed, over the next decade. To me, this is a likelihood with which we must come to grips. The regimes in place lack motivation, a vision for change, and support. The democrats have vision and motivation, but lack support. The Islamists combine all three—motivation, vision, and support. . . . Left to their own devices, the region's discredited regimes are likely to try to muddle through and repress opposition, its budding democrats are likely to fall on their faces, and its extreme Islamists can be expected to become the next agents of change.[2]

When expectations from Algeria dwindled, the experts cast about for some other setting where their dire predictions might come true. In the last few years, there has always been some regime said by these experts to be under imminent threat of collapse, some society supposedly ripe for revolt, if not revolution. Terrorist violence, wherever it occurs, is presented as a clear symptom of a deep-seated groundswell. And it is always those regimes closest to the United States that are singled out by the experts as the most endangered species. In particular, many observers have speculated heavily against these three regimes over the past five years:

- Egypt was supposedly in danger of collapse when Islamist terror struck repeatedly in Cairo a few years ago. (In another *Foreign Affairs* article, ominously titled "The Battle for Egypt," a journalist wrote: "For the United States it is impossible not to compare the current situation in Egypt with the one that led to the disastrous fall of the shah of Iran in 1979."[3]) Egypt is the pivot of U.S. policy in the Arab world, the largest Arab recipient of U.S. aid, and a central player in the peace process.

- Speculation next focused upon Saudi Arabia, again in the aftermath of terrorist acts, this time against U.S. targets. Saudi Arabia enjoys a special relationship with the United States, and its oil is vital to the West.

- Most recently, there has been heavy betting against the regime in Bahrain, where there have been clashes between demonstrators and security forces. Bahrain is the base of the U.S. Fifth Fleet in the Gulf.

Yet despite the warnings of the Cassandras, these regimes are still in place. In some places, even the violence—never an accurate measure of the popular mood anyway—has been quelled. One may argue about the long term, where analysis fades into prophecy. But in the operational term, in which governments formulate policy, the existing regimes have held firm, and look likely to hold firm.

And this is true not only of regimes that are clients of the United States. It is also true of those that are not. When an American president called upon the "Iraqi people" to rise up and cast off the regime of Saddam Hussein, it was a plea of stunning naïveté. There was a Shiite rebellion; even at Saddam's weakest, he was able to suppress it. Saddam still rules today. From various quarters, expert voices are occasionally raised claiming that sanctions against Iraq, Libya, and Iran, were they applied with sufficient rigor, would push their rulers over the brink. As it is, all three regimes—the nemeses of U.S. policy in the region—are reputed to be in economic peril. And yet they remain firmly entrenched in power, with no end to their rule—or their various crimes and misdemeanors—in sight.

UNDERSTATING THE STATE

Where did so many experts go wrong? They understated the power of the state in the Middle East. Looking at the Middle Eastern state, it is easy to see why. In most respects, these states are not models of legitimacy or efficiency. They are ruled by a handful of people—some are presidents, some are kings and sultans, and nearly all of them are rulers for life. The representative institutions that do exist are mechanisms of control rather than governance. Their economies are stagnant, weighed down by cumbersome bureaucracies and drained by corruption. In short, they look much like the Ottoman Empire looked to European observers a century ago: like so many "sick men," whose terminal illness has reached a critical stage.

But it turns out that these regimes have hidden resources and strengths. They are linked to elites, groups, sects, families, and tribes that have a strong vested interest in their continued rule, and that are willing to do whatever is necessary to preserve it. Beneath the massive inefficiencies of the state, there are very efficient security services that know how to ferret out opponents of the existing order. Many of the rulers, especially monarchs whose claims rest upon a combination of descent and Islam, enjoy a legitimacy invisible to outsiders but omnipresent for their subjects.

And above all, there is the absence of legitimate opposition. In Eastern Europe and Latin America, populist movements demanded the replacement of authoritarianism with democratic governance. They enjoyed moral credibility, wide public support and foreign sympathy. In the Middle East, opposition has taken the form of Islamist movements. These seek to substitute one kind of authoritarianism for another. Their programs contain repressive elements that limit their public appeal, and their willingness to use violence strikes fear in many hearts. Despite the apologies made for them by some Western academics, they enjoy scarcely any sympathy in the wider world. In short, they are neither legitimate nor efficient, and their weaknesses are a source of abiding strength for the existing regimes.[4]

And where is "civil society"—that body of concerned citizenry, organized on the basis of interests, whose peaceful interaction is the basis of democracy? There are chambers of commerce, some political parties, a few human rights groups. But civil society is not dense on the ground. What is dense are primordial allegiances—to family, tribe, sect—which are exclusive rather than inclusive, and which offer consistent and dependable support to each individual. The Middle Eastern state has become quite effective at manipulating these allegiances for its purposes, and they are often its most reliable props. This interaction is the key to understanding the resilience of the existing order. While American social scientists, and the foundations which fund them, rush about in search of the familiar landmarks of civil society, real politics happen elsewhere.

For the present, the fact of state power may be taken as a given. What choices does this suggest to the makers of choices? In relation to friendly regimes, it suggests this: do not sell your clients short, do not underestimate the resources at their disposal for the maintenance of their power. This principle might seem obvious, but it is not. Given the craving among academic experts for basic political change in the Middle East, they will always be urging governments to promote political participation, human rights, democratic enlargement, civil society, or whatever other slogan is current.

An ideological policy of the kind urged by academics may look appealing as a rudder for post-Cold War foreign policy. But in Middle Eastern waters, such a rudder can only run the policy ship aground. The obstacles to the fundamental transformation of domestic politics in the Middle East are wide and deep. This is why every great power that has successfully defended its interests in the Middle East has adapted itself to the way politics are practiced there, from the Romans to the British. They exercised a profound influence on the Middle East in many areas. But in governance they left hardly a trace.

Is it really conceivable that the United States will succeed where the others have failed? The record so far is discouraging. The last time a

U.S. administration tried to impose a fundamental change upon a client's way of governing, the client went under. The Shah fell for many reasons, but one was his belief that the United States had abandoned him by making human rights the pivot of policy. The result was an Islamic revolution at least as contemptuous of human rights as the Shah, and still impossible to reconcile with U.S. interests almost 20 years later. Islamic Iran has served as a continuing reminder of the hazards of an ideological policy, of trying to export foreign norms of government.

The promotion of democratic transformation in the Middle East remains an appropriate mission for foundations, endowments, research centers, and Jimmy Carter. They have no interests to preserve and nothing to lose by failure. It is a dangerous mission for government. And in this respect, it has to be said that the makers of U.S. policy have largely resisted the siren calls of democracy theorists. They have preferred to invest their efforts in the Arab-Israeli peace process, where the United States has enjoyed some success. A great power can build bridges between its Middle Eastern clients. Only at its peril does it attempt to remake those clients in its own image.

HEDGING BETS

But why not hedge bets by putting out lines to opposition forces? On the face of it, this would seem the perfectly pragmatic way to reduce the risks of change. It is common diplomatic practice in most of the world. American diplomats and government analysts, ever mindful of the Iranian precedent, would make it common practice in the Middle East as well: they remain fearful of being caught short in a crisis, and so constantly press for latitude to conduct "dialogue" with opposition forces, especially Islamists. Here is one example from the mid-1980s, in congressional testimony by a former U.S. ambassador to Egypt:

> We must develop new modes of diplomacy, potentially involving Islamic leaders, for possible use in crises situations. During the Carter Administration, efforts were made by President Carter to persuade estimable Islamic leaders, respected by Khomeini, to intercede with the Ayatollah for the release of the hostages. It did not work because no

Islamic leader could be found with the stature to confront Khomeini on an Islamic level or a willingness to stick his neck out for the U.S. But this type of contingency, i.e., soliciting intercession on an Islamic level, should be kept in mind and planned for well in advance. Hence, the desirability of sustaining close and constant dialogue with senior Islamic figures everywhere.[5]

And here is more recent advice, dated earlier this year, from a former undersecretary of state for Near Eastern affairs:

Provide opportunities for political activists, including Islamist activists, to meet with American politicians and analysts, even if such meetings displease ruling regimes. That kind of networking, particularly in the countries with smaller populations, can be very useful in establishing personal links that could be important in times of crisis and transition. . . . When Ayatollah Khomeini came to power in Iran, he was an unknown figure to Washington. That kind of thing should not happen again.[6]

One can well understand the desire of foreign policy professionals to cover themselves. Many were pilloried for the debacle in Iran, and not always fairly. But their pleas for dialogue are profoundly misleading.

They mislead by suggesting that an established link to Islamist oppositionists could have made a difference in U.S.-Iranian relations, and might obviate or meliorate a future clash with successful Islamists elsewhere. As it happens, there was a Western government that had precisely such a link to Khomeini and his followers. France admitted Khomeini during the lead-up to the Iranian revolution. It was from a Paris suburb that he conducted his campaign against the Shah. When he returned to Iran, an Air France jet carried him home. The French, by their hospitality and solicitude, were absolutely certain that they would enjoy an inside track with the revolutionary regime.

Did they? Over the next few years, their troops were blown up in Beirut by Iran's clients; their nationals were abducted in Lebanon at Iran's behest; Iranian assassins wantonly killed dissidents on their territory.

Agents of Iran even subjected Paris to a bombing campaign, which prompted the so-called war of the embassies, during which both countries laid siege to one another's embassies. In short, the French got the same treatment as the Americans, if not worse, despite a policy that had effectively coddled the Islamists on their march to power.

The United States too, coddled some Islamists—the so-called Afghan Arabs, whose struggle against the Soviets in Afghanistan enjoyed U.S. support. Even today, it is widely believed in the Arab world that the United States itself created much of the Islamist momentum by its support of these elements. Did the success of this joint effort with the Afghan Arabs win the United States their enduring gratitude? Quite the opposite: they immediately wheeled around after their Afghan success, demonizing the United States and inspiring the worst instance of foreign terrorism on American soil, the World Trade Center bombing. The foreign policy professionals claim that by "dialogue," they want only "to cushion the impact of the Islamist revolution that will come."[7] There is no precedent to sustain the argument that dialogue is capable of achieving anything of the sort.

The plea for dialogue is misleading on a second count. It suggests that such contacts can proceed either without the knowledge of the powers-that-be or with their acquiescence. Neither is possible in the Middle East. All such contacts will eventually become known to the regimes, and will provoke crises of confidence. A few years back, it became known that U.S. embassy officials in Cairo had been in contact with persons affiliated with the Islamic Group, the violent opposition to the Mubarak regime. When the contacts became known after the fact, the news created what Egypt's leading daily called a "silent crisis" between Egypt and the United States.[8] The dialogue also gave a moral boost to the Islamists. "The Mubarak regime is weak," said one Islamist participant in the contacts, "and it is our impression that the Americans are beginning to realize this."[9]

In the Middle East, it is impossible to maintain such contacts and plead innocent. In this part of the world, contacts with opposition forces are something cultivated only against one's enemies. When foreign policy professionals conceal or minimize this fact, they ignore one of the cardinal truths about domestic politics in the Middle East: there is no middle ground.

At best, then, dialogue is useless; at worst, it undermines the morale of clients and emboldens their enemies. And it must be said that the United States, in the last few years, has drawn just this conclusion, backing out of such compromising dialogues. There are many areas in which the United States has found a way to balance its Middle Eastern commitments, most notably in its relations with Israel and Arab states. Between states, even hostile ones, it is possible to open a middle ground, because states have use for effective mediators in their conflicts. But the one thing states will not tolerate is the attempt by foreign powers to establish themselves as mediators in their domestic affairs—efforts which they are bound to regard as hostile intervention.

A serving American diplomat has called precisely for this, urging the United States to "put some moral distance between ourselves and those regimes," and

> . . . make a more convincing case than we have—in our public policy statements, economic and technical assistance programs, and exchange programs—that we do support change through reform, that we care about the welfare of the disadvantaged, and that we do oppose the venal and corrupt practices of the regimes in question, even though we do work with them in pursuit of specific interests. In these situations, to the extent possible, our statements, programs, and assistance should be addressed to peoples, not regimes.[10]

Whether the "peoples" really desire this is far from certain. What is certain is that this is a formula for the erosion of U.S. influence over those who do exercise power, and who have successfully shown their determination to keep it against all challengers. Those rulers who have faced down radical Islamists, coup plotters, and assassins are hardly likely to flinch before an American ambassador or an AID (Agency for International Development) official. The state is still stronger than society in the Middle East, and to bet against it is to defy the odds. American leaders should know that the experts have misrepresented these odds before, and are perfectly capable of misrepresenting them again.

There is much talk among foreign policy professionals about the need for a consistent policy, a policy without hypocrisy and double standards. How can the United States speak of democracy, yet support the kinds of regimes it supports? But consistency on this issue would not build American credibility in the Middle East. After all, in the Middle East itself, the gap between principle and practice, rhetoric and realpolitik, can be breathtaking. There is only one form of consistency that earns genuine respect: you are respected for rewarding your clients and punishing your adversaries. It is in the nature of this divided region that there will be places where the United States is liked, and places where it is detested. But it should be everywhere respected.

CONTAINING ROGUES

There is another side to the enduring power of the state in the Middle East. What is true of client regimes is also true of hostile regimes: they are fixtures. Those who rule Iraq, Libya, and Iran benefit from the same structural advantages as those who rule Egypt, Jordan, and Morocco.

Once upon a time, the United States had a wider range of options in dealing with rogues. It could try to bring them down through cooperation with opposition groups. But coup-making today is as outmoded as the gunboat. Middle Eastern regimes have too many defenses on their perimeters, too many impenetrable layers around their cores. The American resort to sanctions—policies of "containment"—is an attempt to lay siege to these well-fortified regimes.

The objective of containment should not be the toppling of regimes, even less the transformation of the domestic politics of rogue states. Their regimes and systems are as deep-rooted as anywhere else in the Middle East, and attempts to uproot them would prove futile. In their domestic affairs, these states do not represent a much greater affront to American values than client states represent. Iran is not a liberal place, but neither is Saudi Arabia. Iraq and Libya are ruled by nasty men, but these polities are impossible to hold together without an iron hand, and the differences between them and most other Arab polities are of a degree, not of a kind. The issue for the United States is not whether or not the rogues respect human rights. The issue is whether or not they are prepared to follow policies that respect U.S. interests.

For example, it should be immaterial to U.S. policy whether Iran's elections are free or not, whether a new president turns a new leaf for women or not. Of course these things deserve to be monitored by the nongovernmental organizations that build dossiers on elections and human rights. But the U.S. government has the weightier responsibility of defending and advancing its interests. An Iran that actively seeks to undermine U.S. policy and prestige in the region—especially in areas like the Arab-Israeli peace process, where U.S. achievements remain fragile—such an Iran invites containment. This is the one test of consistency on which American credibility does rest, among clients and adversaries alike.

"GONE ARE THE DAYS. . . ."

Might the domination by the state be nearing its end? The theorists have their theories—and usually, they are Rorschach tests for their own preferences. Their debates continue to rage. To an American leader or the maker of an American policy, they are probably irrelevant. But certain arguments about underlying trends do occasionally creep into the margins of policy debates, and deserve critical scrutiny.

It used to be said that runaway population growth, combined with stagnant or negative economic growth rates, would undermine the Middle Eastern state, eventually making it ungovernable. The problem remains acute. In the Arab countries, for example, the 15 years between 1980 and 1994 saw population increase by 50 percent and gross domestic product grow by only 15 percent. Islamist opposition thrived precisely in this gap. But in many Middle Eastern countries, birth rates are leveling off and even decreasing, and some Middle Eastern economies are beginning to register significant growth rates. The prospects for more balanced growth now look rather better than they did a few years ago—a trend that can only strengthen the state.

American observers who long for change have now fixed their hopes on technology. "Gone are the days when government controlled the news," gushes one American professor.

> In Cairo, Damascus, Algiers, or Baghdad, international
> radio and television signals penetrate government censor-

ship and bring images of the world that confound govern-
ment-approved versions. . . . Access to modern communications technology such as computer e-mail—which inherently undermines vertical structures of control—is growing. . .
. The proliferation of printing ateliers and corner shop pho-
tocopy machines ensures that people have more to read than
government-dominated newspapers. Popularly oriented
political tracts and religious pamphlets are readily available
from street vendors.[11]

This belief in the liberating impact of information technology is echoed
by an American diplomat:

What is new is the mobility of information, ideas, and persons. Societies are no longer hermetically sealed. Even the
disadvantaged have access to regional radio and television,
polemical cassette tapes, and, in some cases, international
satellite transmissions. They know that, in other countries
around the world, there is the opportunity of a better life
through individual effort. And, through these same media,
they know that they are not the only ones in their region
suffering their fate.[12]

There is something peculiarly American in this faith in the liberating
influence of technology. But all technology has two faces, no technology is inherently democratizing, and the rulers have not been lax in
mustering information technology for their own ends. People hungry
for information put up satellite dishes—but governments pay to put up
the satellites and jam them with programming. People buy computers
to link up with global networks—but governments restrict access or
maintain the phone lines in ways that restrict the flow of data to a trick-
le. The most efficient and sophisticated systems in the Middle East are
the ones imported by regimes themselves for purposes of domestic
security and surveillance. Satellites and computers, like the printing
press and radio, may yet prove to be one more addition to the toolbox
of authoritarian rule. If an Orwellian scenario for the development of
information technology is feasible anywhere in the world today, it is in
the Middle East.

At this moment, there is no development on the horizon that credibly threatens to diminish the state. The biological clocks of many of the leaders are winding down, but it would be wrong to assume too much from the absence of formal rules of succession or heirs apparent. Regimes have their ways of perpetuating themselves beyond their founders. In Algeria and Iran, in Turkey and Saudi Arabia, there are centers of power, and they have held. Such centers of power now also exist in Syria and Jordan, Libya and Egypt, Morocco and Iraq. There is every prospect that they, too, will hold.

AMERICA'S MOMENT

America's moment in the Middle East coincides with the era of the omnipresent state.

No outside power can choose its moment in the Middle East or the circumstances which prevail there when it arrives. Britain's moment began with the breakup of a 400-year-old empire. At that turning point, history became fluid. British agents like T. E. Lawrence made revolts, and British diplomats like Mark Sykes drew lines on maps that survive to this day.

Many American experts on the region envy the free hand the British had to remake the Middle East. The borders cannot be redrawn now, perhaps with the exception of the borders of Palestine. Yet in one respect Britain failed: in imparting democracy. It is here where many would hope the United States might make its mark. An American diplomat has argued that "one way or another, change is coming," and that "we have reached another turning point in the history of the region."[13]

But all the evidence suggests that the Middle East has managed to evade the turn. If so, it is pointless to lament what cannot be. The American moment in the Middle East has to be used imaginatively for another purpose. The Arab-Israeli conflict may have reached at least a bend in the road, and recent years have given the United States a chance to finish this bit of unfinished business left behind by the British retreat. The restoration of Kuwait to independence also constituted a crucial contribution to the final stabilization of the state system, building a wall where Britain had drawn a line.

To judge from these instances, the opportunities that history has presented to the United States lie in the promotion of stability. *Stability* is a mundane word. No one ever gained the fame of a T. E. Lawrence by advancing and enhancing it. But stabilizing the Middle East is perhaps the essential precondition for all other progress—economic, social, and finally political. It was an American naval strategist, not a British one, who first coined the term *Middle East* a century ago. It is now the only alternative to the idea of the Arab and Islamic world—an idea based on exclusivist identities that can only perpetuate ethnic and religious conflict. In building Middle Eastern stability, in strengthening the state system, strong states are crucial assets. It would be a mistake to cast them aside in pursuit of a romance.

ENDNOTES

1   Robin Wright, "Islam, Democracy and the West." *Foreign Affairs* 71, no. 3 (Summer 1992): 136.

2   "Political Islam: Myths, Realities, and Policy Implications." Speech delivered to the Salzburg Conference of NEA Public Affairs Officers, 21 Sept. 1993.

3   Stanley Reed, "The Battle for Egypt," *Foreign Affairs* 72, no. 4 (September-October 1993): 95.

4   On the character of Islamism, see Martin Kramer, "Ballots and Bullets: Islamists and the Relentless Drive for Power," *Harvard International Review* 19, no. 2 (Spring 1997): 16-19, 61-62. For a detailed critique of Western representations of Islamism, see Martin Kramer, "The Mismeasure of Political Islam," in *The Islamism Debate,* ed. Martin Kramer (Tel Aviv: The Moshe Dayan Center for Middle Eastern and African Studies, 1997), 161-73.

5   Prepared statement of Hermann Fr. Eilts, 24 June 1985, Subcommittee on Europe and the Middle East of the Committee on Foreign Affairs, U.S. House of Representatives, *Islamic Fundamentalism and Islamic Radicalism* (Washington: Government Printing Office, 1985), 71.

6   Richard W. Murphy and F. Gregory Gause, III, "Democracy and U.S. Policy in the Muslim Middle East," *Middle East Policy* 5, no. 1 (January 1997): 64-65.

7   "Political Islam."

8   Salamah Ahmad Salamah, "The United States and Extremism," *Al-Ahram,* 17 April 1993.

9   Chris Hedges, "U.S. Aides in Egypt Said to Have Met With Group Tied to New York Blast," *New York Times,* 23 April 1993.

10 "Political Islam."

11 Augustus Richard Norton, "The Challenge of Inclusion in the Middle East," *Current History* 94 (January 1995): 1.

12 "Political Islam."

13 Ibid.

MEMORANDUM FOR THE PRESIDENT

From: Olivier Roy

**Subject: What You Should Know about Islam as a
Strategic Factor**

1. Do not take Islam at its own words.

Whatever Muslims say about their religion, they tend to be very
assertive (Islam is this or that, allows this or not). They stress the unity
of the Muslim world and its common concerns. It is a usual vision of
Islam that it is an all-encompassing religion, dealing with all aspects of
human life, not separating politics and religion, ethics and law,
rituals and moral behavior. One of the consequences of this self-
assertiveness is that Islam can be integrated only with difficulty into
the patterns of a modern, Western-dominated world, and might even
remain in a permanent state of hostility and confrontation. This perception is shared by many orientalists, especially of the old school. But
in fact, the diversity of the Muslim world does not fit with these statements. The diversity is obvious in history, culture, and geography.
Indonesian politics cannot be explained by the same paradigms used
for Morocco or Syria. Usually when one speaks about the "Islamic
factor" in politics, one focuses on the Middle East and attributes to
Islam what is in fact an Arab paradigm. Islam is seen through the
Middle Eastern prism. But Arabs account for less than 20 percent of the
Muslim ummah, or community. The reverse is also true: Middle
Eastern politics should not be seen through the Islamic prism. Many
actors are not known for their Islamic credentials (from Hafez al-Assad
to Saddam Hussein), and, as we shall see, nationalism is a stronger factor than religion (Palestinian, Syrian, and Egyptian Christians are as
opposed to Israeli colonization on the West Bank, Golan, and Gaza as
their Muslim fellow citizens). The gap between Shiites and Sunnis has
increased since the Iranian Islamic revolution: sectarian feuds have
flared up in Pakistan, Turkey, Iran, Afghanistan. The wave of Islamic
radicalism has in fact increased the fault lines in the Muslim world.

Of course the political actors in the Middle East cannot ignore Islam as a factor of legitimization and try to make use of it—but there are many uses of Islam. The Islamists turn Islam into a more or less radical political ideology, while ruling authorities tend to enlist clerical circles in order to maintain their power, and pay them back by Islamizing a part of the judiciary and the teaching system. A huge part of the population join nonpolitical religious brotherhoods (especially in Egypt, Turkey and Morocco) which provide them with both a communal and spiritual life. Many Muslims have a very secular way of life, and their conservative values have more to do with Middle Eastern culture than religion. The problem is that this real diversity of Islam is not acknowledged by the actors, who all claim that there is one Islam, thus giving an image of a unique world and, in parallel, creating a tension between the ideal of unity and the real and multiple divisions of the Muslim world. This discrepancy does explain the gap between shows of unity (both official, like the Islamic Conference Organization, or popular, like demonstrations in favor of Saddam Hussein in Morocco and Pakistan) and the very lack of concrete solidarity. This myth of Islamic unity has a secular translation: the elusive Arab unity. Hence a typical paradigm of Middle Eastern politics: a permanent sense of instability coupled with a de facto long-term stability interrupted with violent crisis.

The solidarity of the Muslim world has little impact in strategic terms: Afghanistan under Soviet occupation got little support; Palestine, outside the regional states, is an emotional issue which does not alter the strategic constraints of the Muslim states; the Iranian revolution had little long-term impact on other Muslim states (outside the Shi'a communities). During the Gulf war, each state pursued its own interests. The Islamic factor is not obvious even for states who claim to make Islam their main priority. Iran has close relations with Russia, Armenia, and India, against "fellow" Muslim countries like Turkey, Azerbaijan, and Pakistan, although it pretends to promote the worldwide interests of the ummah, the community of Muslims everywhere. All the states surrounding Israel had, at one time or the other, undermined the Palestinian movement in order to prevent it from becoming autonomous.

2. But be sensitive to what Muslims think about their religion.

The myth of the ummah has a tremendous symbolic and psychological impact, hence the discrepancy between the lack of power of the Muslim states and the ability for emotional mobilization (demonstrations, "Death to America," burning of flags, inflammatory speeches, and then . . . back to normal). But even if the myth of the ummah has no effective political effects, it has many symbolic and psychological side effects. Most Muslims do not see Islam as a dominating religion on the move. On the contrary, they perceive Islam as being under pressure and attacks: the failure to unite is rarely attributed to domestic problems (nor to the fact that we are in a world caught between globalization and nation-states, and are not experiencing a clash of civilizations); Muslim public opinion usually attributes the failure of the unity on foreign plots or domestic treachery. There is a sharp contrast between this "suffering Islam" and the image of a "conquering Islam" carried on by Western media. It explains why the reaction from part of the Muslim community is not properly understood (even if it has to be condemned): for example, the Rushdie case appeared first among conservative Pakistani immigrants in Great Britain, who tried to attract the support of the Christian church in a campaign against "blasphemy" in whatever religion. They saw their action as defensive and, paradoxically, as a way to establish a bridge between the great monotheistic religions. Needless to say, what followed did not improve the interfaith dialogue, nor the public image of the Muslim community.

The predicament in the Middle East is that Muslim states are unable and unwilling to push for a common strategy, but cannot unconditionally align themselves with the West without fueling domestic protest and dissatisfaction which has many other causes (social, economic, and political). Mubarak has to deal with a nationalist public opinion. Some Muslim pro-Western States, like Pakistan and Saudi Arabia, even fuel the wave of re-islamization by giving support to movements and networks which might turn against the West (like the so-called Afghans). For them it is a way to maintain both a pro-Western strategic alliance and militant Islamic credentials, which might turn into a gross contradiction: while Western attention is focused against terrorist states, it might appear sooner or later that the terrorists are actually among us and are our friends.

The consequence is that the appeal to Islam will not change the political landscape, but is strong enough to prevent long-term stability.

3. Radical Islam has turned into "Islamonationalism".

The reasons Islam turned into a mobilizing political factor are still there. First was the economic crisis and the tremendous demographic changes which occurred in the Middle East during the 1970s and 1980s (fourfold population increase in most of the big cities, rural migration, fall in oil prices). Second, the crisis of secular ideologies, corruption, and lack of democracy prevented the existing states from providing an adequate answer to these problems. Third, many conservative states, as we saw, fueled the Islamization process themselves (including the Turkish Army in 1982-1983) in order to fight leftist movements. Except in the case of Turkey (since the Erbakan government), the other "anti-Islamist" regimes are still playing on Islamization, or unable to resist it (such as Egypt). This appeal to Islam has been fueled among educated circles by frustration toward the West: in Turkey because of the European ambivalence toward Turkish candidacy to the European Union, in Egypt and Jordan because of the failure of the peace process.

But this steady appeal of Islam among a frustrated intelligentsia, a traditional middle class, and uprooted new city dwellers, has little strategic impact. Most of the Islamist movements have turned into Islamonationalist movements.

Stressing the need to establish a true Islamic state is the common point in all Islamist movements, first in the existing Muslim countries, then beyond them, in order to unite the ummah into a new universal political entity that could challenge Western supremacy. But after some 30 years of Islamist militancy, the picture is quite different from what was expected. Almost all Islamist movements have become nationalist. They have a purely national basis and are expressing a virulent nationalism in more or less religious terms. Hamas challenges Arafat's PLO not on Islam but for "betraying" the national interests of the Palestinian people. Iran has a purely nationalist strategic approach with the region: it supports Christian Armenia against Azerbaijan and did not establish links with the mainstream Sunni Arab Islamist movements (like the Muslim Brethren) because they are too close to Arab nationalism (as shown by their support for Iraq during the first Gulf War). Turabi is using Islam as a tool for unifying Sudan, by Islamizing the Southern Christians and Pagans. The Yemenite Islah movement has been active in the reunification of Yemen, against the wishes of its Saudi godfather. The Lebanese Hezbollah is now stressing the defense of the Lebanese nation and has established a working relationship with many Christian circles. The Turkish Refah Party, by stressing the Ottoman heritage, is trying to affirm a kind of neo-Ottoman Turkish leadership in the Middle East. By the same token, the Shi'a radical parties of Iraq, like Dawa', are stressing the need for national unity and are working closely with non-Islamic national parties.

The combination of nationalism, populism and the call for morality and authenticity is the source of the influence of Islamist movements on domestic issues, but, once in power, the movements' leaders have little room for changing the society or the strategic environment. The Islamists sooner or later need to find a compromise not only with the West, but with Westernization. The repression against women appears when women enter educational and job markets, but this trend cannot be reversed. For instance, the war against Iraq has altered gender patterns in Iran by bringing women into the labor force. Everywhere, from Algeria to Iran, extended families are giving way to smaller units. The age gap between spouses is shortening. In a way, the Muslim world is now affected by a profound sociological and cultural "modernization," which also means Westernization. Reaction in the name of authenticity and the call to fight "Western cultural aggression" are not very successful, as we can see in Iran, where there is a popular call for a more open society.

Confronted with the realities of power, Islamic movements are in fact unable to provide a new model for social and economic justice. They soon tend to revert to non-Islamic patterns of ruling the country: choosing either a statist economy as in Iran during the eighties, or a liberal and free trade market, as advocated by the FIS and many clerical Iranian leaders (Nategh Nouri). Most of their achievements are on mores, law, and daily life. Iran, Taliban's Afghanistan, and Saudi monarchy are close as far as their conception of daily Islam is concerned (veil and shariat), but they are dealing with very different societies and have very different strategic perspectives of their interests. Islam as such is not a strategic factor.

In the present circumstances (given the failure of the peace process), the prospect is further extension of Islamonationalist movements— anti-Western, but acting within their own national strategic constraints. There is in fact little comparison with the "Arab nationalism" of the 1960s. Islam is a new flag for old antagonisms; it does not change the global picture. Terrorism is by no means an Islamic by-product: terrorist states and organizations in the 1970s were secular, such as the Palestinian FPLP, the Abu Nidal group, Syria, Iraq.

4. Islam and violence.

One can find something in the Koran and in the writings of the recognized commentators on the Koran and the Sunna to justify almost anything in political terms, from having good relations with the Jews or fighting them, living peacefully with nonbelievers or trying to convert them, making jihad a very exceptional and temporary enterprise, or calling for a permanent holy war. Islamist radicals tend to quote (more or less accurately, by the way) the more rigid commentators, like Ibn Taymiyya, while moderates find more lenient views elsewhere. The problem is that, since the 1970s, there has been an almost hegemony of radical views, not in the mind but from the most vocal of the pulpits. The moderates are squeezed between radical Islamists and the official conservative Islam of the ruling regimes, even when the latter are pro-Western. The "official" brand of Islam, including in "secular" states like Turkey, is usually conservative, hostile to a cultural Western influence, and not open to pluralism and debate.

The liberal Muslim thinkers used to settle in Western countries in order to avoid pressure not only from radicals but also from nondemocratic regimes, including, once again, "anti-Islamist" ones, like Algeria, Egypt, and others. But, in the West, there is a general misunderstanding between many of the moderate Muslim intellectuals and the Western media and political circles, who still press upon them for "secular" statements about issues which have nothing or little to do with Islam. One can be a liberal Muslim (or even a Christian Arab like Edward Saïd) and a critic of the peace process or of the Gulf War.

Violence in the Middle East is not directly connected with Islam, although the latter might provide legitimization, and solace for the sacrifices. Palestinian terrorism was secular two decades ago (as in the neo-Marxist PLFP). Terrorist states might also be secular (Syria, Iraq, and recently Algeria, for the killing of Mecili in Paris). The violence in the Middle East comes from political, national, and strategic indigenous problems, not from Islam, or even radical Islam as such. It is useless to point to Islamic "rogue states" while many actors in the political violence, from Sheykh Omar Abdurrahman, sentenced for the bombing of the World Trade Center, to the founders of the rebel movement in Algeria, had been trained with Saudi, Pakistani, and American support to fight the Soviets in Afghanistan.

With the exception of Palestine, where terrorism is linked with Palestinian nationalism, true ideological radicalization might come mainly from splinter groups or outcasts, who dream of a universal ummah but have neither state nor country to claim as their own. While terrorist actions in the 80s have been strategically and ideologically motivated (in order to force the Western countries to change their strategy in the Middle East), most terrorist actions in the present decade have no strategic prospects and have been perpetrated by rootless militants (like Ramzi for the World Trade Center, and Kelkal for the bombings in France in 1995). These networks might be used here or there by state secret services and might perpetrate bloody actions, but do not seem able to shape a new kind of political mobilization among the Muslim populations.

5. Islam and democracy.

The question is not so much whether Islam is compatible with democracy, but who is really a democrat in the Middle East. The fight against radical Islam, in Egypt, Turkey, Algeria, and Syria, is also a fight against democracy, even, of course, if Islamists are not democrats. But there is a growing sense in these countries that secularism can be maintained only at the expense of democracy, thus pushing toward radical Islam people who simply are not happy about the lack of economic and political perspectives. This also entails the usual accusations of double standards by the West, which closes its eyes to violations of human rights in Algeria, Turkey, Egypt, and even Syria.

The danger for the West is in supporting antidemocratic regimes simply because they are secular, like in Algeria, with the result being an increase in violence and tension. In fact, in countries where the Islamists are given access to the political game, they tend to accept the rules of the game, even if they stick to their ideologies (i.e., Turkey, Jordan, Yemen, Kuwait, and Pakistan). With the exception of small splinter groups, the mainstream Islamists (that is the Muslim Brethren) join armed struggle only when they are violently repressed (Syria). If not, they can be integrated in the political game. Their nationalism in this case prevents any coalition of countries under the Islamic banner and even pits Islamist movements against each other (as seen when the Muslim Brethren from Egypt, Kuwait, and Jordan took very different positions during the Gulf war).

One of the main misconceptions about Islam is that it has to endeavor an intellectual reform process in order to meet the requirements of both modernity and democracy. But the prospects for seeing the emergence of a "reformed Islam" are not very bright. The first problem is the general commitment to the uniqueness of Islam: anybody who claims too loudly that one should reform Islam will be branded as a proponent of "American Islam" (this is an Iranian expression).

The second problem is that the so-called moderate Muslim states (Egypt, Saudi Arabia, and even Turkey) are promoting a conservative Islam, which does not stress convergence between the different religions. Under Mubarak, the different "fatwas" and statements issued by religious authorities or by the official courts are far closer to fundamentalist Islam than those by Gamal Nasser during his time as the archenemy of the West. Different academic institutions, subsidized by the Saudis in order to undercut Islamic radicalism, are also pushing forward a conservative and culturally anti-Western brand of Islam.

The third problem is that Islamic intellectuals living in the West are either cut off from mainstream Muslims because they are perceived as too Westernized, or, on the contrary, held under suspicion by Western circles because they are supposed to be radical. The consequence is a gap between reformers and the religious establishment.

However, this does not mean that Islam is not changing. Adaptation, although it lacks a theoretical framework, is nevertheless taking place in the daily practices of many Muslim circles. In political terms, we saw that when they are not repressed, the mainstream Islamic political parties tend to play the game according to the rules. There is a genuine will among the Muslim Brethren (from Morocco to Egypt, Jordan, and Syria) to become legal political actors and to accept the rules. What we can see is the slow emergence of "Muslim democrats," the same way that a "Christian democracy" (by the way, Pope John Paul is not a democrat) became the cornerstone of politics in many West European countries. This trend is also reenforced by the in situ intellectual evolution of Muslims living in Europe.

6. Islam is also a Western religion, which will lead to a more personal religiosity.

The voluntary settlement of Muslims in non-Muslim lands is altering not the religious basics of Islam but the traditional way of living Islam as an all-encompassing religion. Islam in the West is no longer embedded in daily culture, common law, social pressure, and obvious models of behavior. It has to be reinvented and made personal by individuals.

The "nationalization" of the Middle Eastern Islamist movements promotes a growing gap between them and the Muslims living in non-Muslim societies, mainly in Western Europe and the United States. (Russia is also part of the picture, with some 8 million Muslims.) Links with the countries of origin tend to be loosened or severed after the second or third generation. Muslims are torn between an ethnic identity (Arabs, Turks, etc.) and a religious one (being Muslims above all ethnic and linguistic specificity). In any case, these constructed identities do not fit with the national politics of the countries of origin. Muslims in the West are integrated into the social and political system of the host country, even if they contribute to modifying its political landscape (for example, by calling for the recognition of a "Muslim identity," albeit with little success, even in Great Britain). Paradoxically, the struggle to establish a purely religious identity above ethnic and national origins contributes to the severing of the link between Western Muslims and the country of origin. Muslims in the West are no longer a bridgehead for Middle East politics, as shown by their inability to establish a Muslim lobby.

Islam is a way for recent Muslim immigrants in the West to cast their identity into a purely religious one, in the Western sense of religion, meaning that it is no longer embedded in a given culture and judicial system. They slowly give up the old ethnic or national identity without converting to Christianity or becoming atheist. They want Islam to be put on an equal footing with Christian confessions or Judaism, but in the process they must acknowledge, even unwillingly, that Islam is a mere religion. The simple fact that there is no legal way in the West to impose and enforce the implementation of Islamic rules and norms among the believers creates a process of privatization of religion, meaning that it is a matter of personal choice, not a societal question. Muslim women are free to wear the veil or not. In a context where there is a de facto secularism and where Muslims can simply not ask for legal and forcible implementation of their religious tenets, Islam tends to become more and more a question of faith and individual choice. The question is not how Islam deals with secularism, but how Muslims living voluntarily in a non-Muslim state deal with an overwhelming secularism. And they indeed do it, by stressing values, meanings, and ends instead of the sheer implementation of legal injunctions. In this sense, Islam in the West is no longer an importation.

Islam is changing not in terms of theology or legal interpretation but in terms of religiosity. This process of "secularization" of Islam does not alter the theological framework. It simply shows that Islam can evolve not necessarily as theology but in the way it is experienced by the believers. We should speak no more about Islam, but about Muslims.

MEMORANDUM FOR THE PRESIDENT

From: **Your Staff**

Subject: Summary of Discussion on the Muslim World

This is our summary. It may not necessarily reflect everyone's views, and some may disagree with the conclusions.

1. We can speak of the Muslim world or "Islamdom" as a civilization that grew up and flourished under the aegis of a religion, and that includes countries where the majority of the population are Muslims, such as the 54 states that have joined the Organization of the Islamic Conference. Islam is part of individual loyalties and identities, not just a religious faith. Labeling a country as Islamic or Muslim can, however, be a poor guide for policy analysis. Worse, such labels can mislead. They blur crucial distinctions both among Muslims and among the countries in which they live, from Morocco to Indonesia.

In trying to explain the political behavior and economic performance of Muslim states, we asked ourselves which explanatory variable seemed most powerful. Our tentative impression was that national identities were most powerful, followed by the capacities of the state apparatus. As an explanatory variable, the religious beliefs of the majority population did not appear to be decisive. Even within the Arab world, Muslim or Islamic states do not display any special capacity for collective action in international affairs, though the Arab League is an important forum in which concerns are shared (both in front of and behind the curtain). Islamic beliefs are very important in many ways obvious to anyone who has ever visited a Muslim country. Islam certainly influences national policies, political culture, and the way policies are developed. Yet this importance must be placed in perspective, especially in developing international policies for the United States.

2. There is a growing discrepancy between mainstream Islamic beliefs and the beliefs espoused by radical groups, though such cyclical rifts have a long tradition in Muslim history. Islamic political groups that we may consider extreme in their beliefs or actions may share the search for political empowerment of Islamic beliefs, but they arise out of the

particular context of one or another nation. Also, most Muslims are not "fundamentalists" and most "fundamentalists" are not terrorists. We doubt that groups seeking more Islamic forms of government represent an irresistible tide of mass opinion. The militant fringe groups lack international solidarity. The United States is often a target only in relation to local goals. Some of the more notorious acts of terror directed against Americans come from individuals or groups so marginal and rootless that they have lost a national context for action; what one participant called "stateless soldiers in an imaginary jihad." Washington is better off focusing on states or statelike entities that may espouse such causes in their diverse national interests, as in Sudan or Afghanistan, or that mix such ideals into their political vocabulary and national identities while primarily pursuing unique agendas, as in Libya, Syria, Iran, or factions within the Palestine National Authority.

3. The United States should not have any policy toward Islam per se. It should not give Islam an enemy. Rather the United States should have policies toward states. In that context, U.S. policymakers do need to integrate understanding of religion within foreign policy, overcoming traditional discomfort with this topic.

4. Regionally, we worry about demographic and economic trends in the Arab, Turkish, and Iranian Middle East. Population growth in excess of 3 percent per year will overwhelm almost any economic growth. We also note the pragmatic pressure to integrate women into productive society and the work force and to equalize their access to education. The countries cannot afford economically to exclude so much of the population from educated contributions to development. More broadly, if Muslim states do not allow women to take their place in the social, cultural, and political community, these countries are unlikely to catch up to the modern world.

5. The United States should, and will, view greater democracy, political pluralism, reliance on the rule of law, and free-market economies with sympathy. Yet any direct U.S. policy interventions to achieve such outcomes are more meaningfully considered on a case-by-case basis, building on local models for action. Stability in the Muslim world is a paradox. Threats to stability abound. Yet the states have been remark-

ably strong and durable, with great continuity in the ruling personalities. The states have been so strong precisely because they have been so threatened. In this context, U.S. interventions could easily be counterproductive, limiting the political space for reform, as well as injuring other U.S. policy objectives. American engagement is needed. Yet states in the Islamic world can be better judged by the United States, and held accountable by the United States, for their international behavior.

Further Questions: Is it possible to draw lessons from the Southeast Asian model of Islam for states in North Africa, the Middle East, or South Asia? Are there notable differences, even within South Asia, between the political and economic performance of Muslim communities within Pakistan, India, and Bangladesh?

AMERICA
AND
SAUDI ARABIA

MEMORANDUM FOR THE PRESIDENT

From: **Your Staff**

Subject: Questions for Discussion on America and
Saudi Arabia

1. If the long-standing U.S.-Saudi relationship is founded on oil, how durable is this foundation?

   - Will the danger of supply disruption or increased prices really be serious enough to threaten the vital interests of the United States?

   - Will Saudi Arabia continue to play a unique role as price moderator and supplier of last resort?

2. How sustainable is the Saudi-American (and Gulf Cooperation Council [GCC]) coalition against Iraq in its current form?

   - Goals: Should the allies plainly declare that they will never deal with Saddam Hussein and/or modify the goal or scope of economic sanctions?

   - Means: Is the current force posture of the alliance adequate to the task and sustainable for years to come?

   - Actions: Have American policing operations against Iraq become too costly (as with the October 1994 deployments) or too weak (as in the punitive actions of January 1993 and September 1996, or the current enforcement of UNSCOM disarmament demands under the accord negotiated by UN Secretary General Kofi Annan)?

   - Burden sharing: Is a different balance of responsibilities needed between the United States and Saudi Arabia, between Saudi Arabia and other GCC states, or between the United States and other key oil consumers in Europe and, especially, Asia?

3. How vulnerable is the relationship to arguments within the partnership:

   - Arising from the Arab-Israeli dispute?

- Arising from divergent policies toward Iran?

4. Should the United States take a more active interest in the domestic governance of Saudi Arabia?

  - What would be the operational objectives of such a policy for either political reform or economic development?

  - Should the United States distance itself from the interests of the royal family?

MEMORANDUM FOR THE PRESIDENT

From: Robert Satloff

Subject: What about Saudi Arabia Should (or Shouldn't) Concern You

Source of General Concern: *U.S. ignorance about Saudi domestic politics and challenges to Saudi domestic security.*

Among countries in the world whose security the United States is pledged to defend, U.S. officials probably know the least about events and trends inside Saudi Arabia. In the past, when the Saudis faced only episodic threats to internal stability, such as the takeover of the Grand Mosque at Mecca, reconciling this imbalance was neither too difficult nor too troubling. Today, however, as noted below, circumstances have changed, leading to genuine concern about the political fate of the Saudi kingdom. In short, Washington cannot be confident that it has adequate knowledge and information about Saudi Arabia, that it knows either the substance or the process of Saudi decision making, or that it even "knows what it doesn't know" about politics within the ruling family, within the religious establishment and the emerging Islamic opposition, within the armed forces and National Guard, and within various other segments of society (tribes, intellectuals, the business community, etc.). It was this sense of concern that recently prompted the Central Intelligence Agency to establish a special task force dedicated to following Saudi domestic developments. Finding disinterested sources of information on Saudi Arabia, outside the traditional channels of diplomatic or business contact, should be of high concern to U.S. policymakers.

Source of Immediate Concern: *The threat of terrorism against U.S. interests and personnel in Saudi Arabia.*

Twenty-five U.S. soldiers have been killed in Saudi Arabia in two terrorist attacks in the past two years, equaling nearly one-fifth the total number of U.S. soldiers killed by Iraqis throughout Desert Storm.[1] While terrorism may not pose an existential threat to Saudi stability, it does pose a very real threat to U.S. forces deployed in Saudi Arabia and, by extension, to the will and ability of the United States to defend Saudi Arabia. Specifically, terrorism poses the following problems: (1) that local commanders divert significant resources toward the defense against terrorism and are, in the process, distracted from their principal mission—preparing for defense against conventional, external military aggression;[2] (2) that at some point, the U.S. "home front" tires of the human price involved in maintaining a ground presence in Saudi Arabia and demands its recall or removal off-shore;[3] (3) that the Saudi government, acting under (perceived) pressure from public opinion, may decide that the domestic political costs of continued U.S. deployment outweigh its benefits. All three of these problems, or combinations thereof, could have serious, negative repercussions for long-term U.S. interests in the region.

Source of Immediate Concern: *The obvious needs restatement—the Gulf war is not over; there is simply a cease-fire.*

Factors which led to the U.S. deployment of a half-million troops to Saudi Arabia have not disappeared. Indeed, with Saddam Hussein still in power, continuing to flout UN resolutions regarding weapons of mass destruction and missile delivery systems whenever he can, Saudi and U.S. leaders must view seriously the threat of Iraqi adventurism; indeed, hostilities in the Gulf could flare up, in any number of ways, without much warning. Despite the temporary resumption of UNSCOM inspections under the accord negotiated by Kofi Annan, the potential of war should be of great concern to senior U.S. officials and the prospect, while significantly diminished as a result of Desert Storm and U.S. vigilance since then, nonetheless remains real and present. While Saddam's demise will not end the Iraqi threat to Saudi Arabia, there will almost surely remain a threat as long as Saddam and his cohorts remain in power in Iraq. Unless the threat which prompted the deployment of U.S. forces to Saudi Arabia is itself reduced to a much smaller level, then thousands of U.S. troops are likely to remain deployed on Saudi soil, with the continual prospect of terrorism outlined above.

Source of General Concern: *Reliance on Saudi Arabia as a stable producer of an increasing amount of the world's oil (both in real and relative terms) is growing, not decreasing.*

According to U.S. Department of Energy (Energy Information Agency) estimates of future global demand and supply, consumers are relying on Saudi Arabia to increase its production from about 8.5 million barrels per day (mbd) to 14.9 mbd by the year 2010—an increase of 76 percent. The Saudis are indeed making impressive gains in identification and extraction technology, with some suggesting that a 14 mbd figure may be reached by the early years of the next decade. However, it must be recalled that attaining this level of capacity is viewed as a *requirement* to meet growing global demand (especially new demand from East and South Asia), not a luxury simply to maintain reasonably low prices. This reliance on Saudi Arabia to increase production capacity is especially critical if current U.S. and UN policies limiting the export of Iraqi oil and limiting the technological development of the Iranian oil industry remain in place.

Source of General Concern: *By any standard of measurement, Saudi Arabia's domestic security is less "stable" today than a decade ago.*

Over the last quarter century, four factors have been at the heart of Saudi domestic stability:

1. Unity of the Al Saud, based on the historical memory of disunity having contributed to the collapse of the monarchy in the 19th century. One product of this familial unity is a succession process that has produced fairly smooth transitions of power among the sons of Ibn Saud despite the circumstances of the transition (ranging from natural death to deposition to assassination).

2. A grand bargain with the Saudi population, by which the kingdom purchased the political quiescence, if not loyalty, of its subjects through an extensive series of commitments regarding social welfare, jobs, education, housing, and other areas. The key to this bargain was the equation of high income and low population.

3. Legitimacy based on the combination of "custodianship" of Mecca and Medina, Islamic orthodoxy, and zealous efforts to prevent the intrusion into Saudi society of Western influences that might undermine it.

4. Monopoly on the forces of coercion in society and little reluctance to use them when necessary.

Today, three of these four factors are under pressure or challenge:

1. Saudi Arabia is about to begin a period of extended succession that has the potential for significant intragenerational as well as intergenerational divisions within the ruling family that could weaken the familial consensus on strategic issues. The succession issue has several aspects to it:

   a. The expected accession of Abdullah, the non-Sudairi senior prince, with the risk that the Sudairis may seek to make an ineffectual Khalid out of Abdullah and Abdullah's own efforts to counter that scheme.

   b. A possible Andropov-Chernenko-type series of short reigns, given that the current crown prince and his expected successor (Sultan) are both in their 70s, approaching the life expectancy of Ibn Saud's sons. A series of brief reigns is likely to produce weak and uncertain leadership.

   c. The eventual intrafamily debate regarding the transfer of succession to the generation of Ibn Saud's grandsons. Once it moves to the next generation it is unlikely to move back, which creates the potential for intense internecine competition.

2. The grand bargain has been under severe strain and may be unraveling. This is the result of two basic factors:

   a. The Saudi population has risen dramatically, due largely to improvement in health care (lowering infant mortality and increasing life expectancy) plus a generally pronatalist governmental policy. While Saudi population statistics are notoriously suspect, certain trends are clear. Saudi population growth averaged around 1.7 percent per year during the 1960s, rose to 2.4 percent during the 1970s, and skyrocketed to 3.5 percent during the decade from the mid-1980s to mid-1990s, with a forecast for a growth rate of 3.6 percent for the period 2000-2010.[4] Already Saudi Arabia has one of the world's highest fertility rates (approximately seven live births) and one of the world's most youthful populations, with approximately 42 percent of the population under the age of 14. While remaining skeptical about the raw statistics, one is truly remarkable—the World Bank has projected the Saudi population in the year 2025 to be nearly 44 million, virtually on par with the population of Iraq, which will be only 48 million!

b. Oil prices are (relatively) low and despite high Saudi production, Saudi GDP has been flat or even shrinking. Indeed, between 1982 and 1994, Saudi Arabia registered negative or zero growth rates 8 out of 13 years. In current dollars, Saudi GDP reached $94 billion in 1981—but that was not reached again until 1990, 9 years later.[5]

These two factors have resulted in a precipitous drop in Saudi per capita GDP, from a high of near $20,000 to its current level of less than $7,000, with direct implications for the living standards of the ordinary Saudi. At first, the government sought to cushion the shock by maintaining virtually all of the social welfare commitments; this, combined with the huge expense of the Gulf war, led to substantial deficit spending for the first time in modern Saudi history.[6] In recent years, the government has begun to take measures to trim expenditure on entitlements (e.g., subsidies, education, health, housing), to retreat on the tacitly recognized commitment to post-college employment for Saudi men, and to slow the pace of payments on government contracts.

The bottom line is that the system developed in the 1970s to ensure quiescence to the Al Saud lacks adequate "lubrication." The result has been the growth of resentment, dissatisfaction, and criticism in various forms—e.g., the still-nascent emergence of politics within a society that has traditionally prevented virtually all forms of political activity. There are many manifestations of this development, including the various petitions which circulated from liberals and Islamic conservatives after the Gulf war. Perhaps the most visible sign that the Saudi regime has recognized this development was the inauguration of the long-promised *majlis al-shura,* recently renewed for a second four-year term with a revamped (though still appointed) membership.

3. A religious-based Sunni political opposition has begun to emerge and make itself felt in various arenas of Saudi society. Such opposition includes members of the religious establishment (reflected in the forced retirement of seven senior ulema shortly after the Gulf war and the creation of two new bureaucratic bodies—including one headed by Defense Minister Prince Sultan—whose raison d'etre is to diminish the religious purview of the existing ecclesiastical authorities) and the younger, more disaffected opposition ulema (reflected in the arrest of 157 Islamic activists in 1994, including two leading opposition ulema). The political challenge posed by some disaffected religious authorities is, perhaps, more significant in the long run for Saudi stability than the near-term challenge posed by the most vocal oppositionists (the fax-happy Committee for the Defense of Legitimate Rights, operating in exile) and small groups of violent Sunni oppositionists (e.g., those implicated in the November 1995 bombing of the OPM-SANG office in Riyadh), about which very little is known.

In most Muslim-majority countries, the relatively mild critiques the Saudis have endured from their dissatisfied ulema would not produce significant concern. However, precisely *because* Saudi legitimacy is defined by the regime's religious credentials and its commitment to Islamic orthodoxy, the very existence of a religious critique from the "right" is a potentially severe blow. In this regard, the Saudis are, to a large extent, being hoisted by their own Islamic petard. Current problems are, at least in part, the product of the regime's past support for Afghan radicals and other Islamic revolutionary movements, its heavy emphasis on Islamic education, its recruitment of Egyptian Ikhwani teachers in Saudi schools, and its deference to Islamic radicals as a political payoff for the kingdom's acceptance of the deployment of U.S. troops during the Gulf war. Whereas the regime has long dealt with problems of disaffection and possible political opposition from the Saudi Shiite population (through a rather effective stick-and-carrot approach), it is particularly significant that the growth of religious-based disaffection is now occurring among the Saudi Sunni population.

4. The fourth factor—monopoly on the forces of coercion—seems largely unchanged. The kingdom has not hesitated to use force against

its opponents (e.g., swift executions of the OPM-SANG accused as well as roundups of Islamic militants) and, to the extent that information is available, there are few signs of disaffection within the armed forces or the Saudi Arabian National Guard (SANG). One unknown, however, will be the role of the SANG and the nature of its leadership and its relationship to the armed forces in the Abdullah and post-Abdullah era.[7]

Individually, each of the three problems outlined above could probably be addressed adequately by the Saudi leadership. What makes the current period acutely difficult is that the regime faces the combination of these problems at the same time. Structurally weak leadership, a soft economy with rising unemployment, and a rise in Islamic opposition could prove to be a combustible mix. It is also an uncertain mix, possibly producing new and significant political alliances (e.g., Islamists and young, ambitious princes).

From this assessment, one should draw the following conclusion: By whatever scale one judges "domestic stability," a lower grade must be given to Saudi Arabia today as compared with a decade ago. This doesn't necessarily mean that Saudi Arabia merits a grade of "unstable"; on the contrary, the regime probably has more staying power than many observers give it credit for. However, stability-related issues are now a much higher concern to Saudi leaders and are likely to occupy Saudi leaders even more in the near- and medium-term.

Even without factoring in the Abdullah-specific aspects of the potential for political change in the kingdom (see below), the focus on internal stability in coming years will have important implications for all aspects of U.S.-Saudi relations, from Saudi Arabia's willingness to remain a major importer of U.S. goods to its support for U.S. political initiatives outside the Gulf. These potential changes in Saudi approaches to the U.S. relationship will be magnified by their apparent contrast from the particularly close political, economic, and strategic ties the two countries have enjoyed throughout much of the 1990s.

Source of General Concern: *Post-Fahd Saudi Arabia is likely to drift away from the overtly pro-United States stances that Fahd has adopted on a number of issues as Abdullah seeks to define himself to be what Fahd is not.*

Prince Abdullah aches to be king, tasted the reins of power when serving as regent during Fahd's illness, and has been promised—but has never received—appointment as prime minister. When his accession finally arrives, he will most likely seek to put his own imprint on the kingdom and its foreign and domestic policies, always watching the efforts of the remaining Sudairi brothers[8] to keep him in check. On core matters, Fahd was pro-American: his willingness to throw Saudi Arabia's lot in with the United States in 1990; his support (strong in Saudi terms, weak in the view of others) for the Arab-Israeli peace process that followed the Gulf war; and his proven willingness to "buy American" over the years. While there is no evidence that Abdullah opposes Fahd's current policy of close alliance with the United States, Abdullah has already indicated his intention to deviate from Fahd's path on a number of policy matters and move toward a more "pan-Arabist" line (a term so far ill-defined). On the peace process, for example, the strong, vocal, and early public stance against Saudi participation in the Doha Middle East/North Africa economic summit conference suggests a harder line on the peace process than was the case under Fahd; indeed, staking out such a stark position three months before any decision needed to be made on the issue was itself "un-Saudi-like." Similarly, on Jordan, Abdullah has reportedly been critical of the Jordan-Israel peace treaty; on Iran, Abdullah has sent signals of his desire to ease tensions at a time when other Saudi officials have been tacitly accusing Tehran of complicity in the Al Khobar bombing.

The core question is the Saudi approach toward the U.S. security relationship. Until 1990, the Saudis preferred the United States remaining "over the horizon," ready to act as a "rescue squad" in the event of a security emergency. Since the Gulf war and the continued deployment of some 5,000 U.S. troops on Saudi soil, the strategy has shifted toward deterrence, with the U.S. seeking to deter aggression rather than standing ready to respond to it. The U.S. and Saudi Arabia seemed to draw further apart, not closer, during the military confrontation with Iraq in early 1998. Whether an Abdullah-led Saudi Arabia would seek to return to the pre-Gulf war approach toward the U.S. security guarantee—without first having attained significant threat reduction (in the form of a change of regime or other force reduction mechanisms in Iraq)—remains a source of concern.

Nonconcerns: *Two scenarios that are often raised in discussions of potential domestic developments in Saudi Arabia are, in reality, "nonconcerns." These are:*

1. The Shah-Khomeini model.

Many factors suggest that the Iranian model of revolutionary change is not applicable to Saudi Arabia. There is no history of mass organized opposition movements or coalitions of opposition groups; no history of clerical aspirations to political rule (though there is a long pattern of clerical partnership with political rulers, as in the Wahhabi-Saudi alliance); no history of political agitation among the business (*bazaari*) class, etc. Other points of contrast include the Saudi claim to religious legitimacy (quite different from the Shah's Persian nationalism) and the regime's lack of compunction to use force to assert its control. In short, while the potential for political change is growing in Saudi Arabia, it is highly unlikely to take the form of a popular revolution.

2. Saudi Shiites as a substantial threat to internal security.

While there is considerable disaffection among Saudi Shiites—generally estimated to constitute about 10 percent of the total population, residing principally in the oil-rich eastern sectors of the country—they do not pose an existential threat to the state. Over the years, the Saudis have crafted a fairly effective strategy of economic "incentives" and political and security "disincentives" that has reduced the potential security challenge from the Shiites. While there is an upsurge in political and even insurrectionary activity among Shiites, almost surely encouraged by Iran (e.g., the activity of Saudi Hezbollah and like-named groups), the revulsion that most Sunnis hold toward Shiites will limit the popular appeal of their efforts. Radical Shiites can be successful in episodic terrorist actions, but they cannot pose a fundamental challenge to the regime. While elements within the regime may at times underscore the threat from radical Shiite groups and their Iranian patrons, a far more serious challenge would be posed by the emergence of a sustained, religious-based Sunni opposition movement.

ENDNOTES

1   In Desert Storm, 146 U.S. troops were killed in action, including 35 from "friendly fire."

2   This was the impression I received from a visit to the U.S. air and army bases in Kuwait in November 1996.

3   It is noteworthy that terrorism against U.S. forces in Saudi Arabia has so far not provoked the sort of "bring the boys home" public outcry that followed the Somalia debacle and that has swirled around the Bosnia deployment from the very beginning.

4   For statistics, see World Bank, *World Development Report,* various annual editions, and Standard and Poor's, *World Economic Outlook,* first quarter 1997.

5   Standard and Poor's, *World Economic Outlook,* first quarter 1997.

6   From 1972 to 1982, the current account was in deficit just once (1978, at a level of $2.2 billion); since then, the current account balance has been in deficit every year.

7   Crown Prince Abdullah is commander of the National Guard, a well-equipped, 60,000-man force that not only provides regime defense but also acquitted itself relatively well in the Gulf War. This force should not be confused with the Saudi Armed Forces, which come under the authority of the Minister of Defense, Prince Sultan.

8   The Sudairi princes, including King Fahd and Defense Minister Sultan, are sons of the regime's founder, Ibn Saud, who are themselves full brothers, i.e., children of the same mother. Abdullah is a half-brother to the Sudairis, the lone son of the union of his mother and Ibn Saud.

MEMORANDUM FOR THE PRESIDENT

From: Abdulaziz H. Al Fahad

Subject: How Saudi Leaders View America and the World

Relative to the turmoil of the Gulf war and its aftermath, these are comparatively tranquil times in Riyadh. The regional situation is reasonably controlled; economic conditions have somewhat improved; and domestic political agitation has been subdued. Yet these same issues, while currently dormant, are not dead nor are they likely to die soon. Recent concerns about the health of the aging King only serve to highlight some of the uncertainties faced by the decision makers in Riyadh.

Barring some unusual development, succession to the King is not a contentious issue in Saudi Arabia for the foreseeable future. The heir apparent and the one following have been designated for some time now, and succession should be orderly as has been demonstrated in the past. Despite concerns over the King's health, all publicly available indications show a smoothly run government and some substantial decisions being made. As recently as July 1997, the Consultative Council, whose term had expired, was enlarged and more than 40 new members named. Still, some fundamental issues have not been dealt with, such as appointments within the Royal family (the tenure of many of whom had expired and was renewed without any changes). Some pressing issues with respect to the economy, especially subsidies and fees for utilities and government services, have been addressed only partially. It is unlikely that many of these issues will disappear— they will ultimately have to be tackled.

The Gulf war of 1990-91 confronted the Saudis with one of their most serious challenges in modern times. The Iraqi occupation of Kuwait forced upon the Saudis unpalatable choices. To leave Saddam Hussein in Kuwait would have exposed them to serious long-term consequences which the country might not have survived. To invite the Americans was an admission of military weakness with serious domestic repercussions. Unpalatable as the choices may have been, the Saudis chose the least evil of the alternatives and invited the Americans to protect the country and to liberate Kuwait. That decision entailed certain consequences, not all of which have been positive. Kuwait has been liberated and Iraq is contained, that is obvious. Yet there are equally serious, negative, if less visible, consequences on the domestic scene.

The Gulf war is rather unusual in the annals of great power interventions. While in the past the great power intervened at its own expense, so to speak, in the Gulf war the "client" states along with other allies had to foot the bill. Some rich allies, notably Germany and Japan, as well as Kuwait and the United Arab Emirates, paid substantial amounts to the United States. But it was only the Saudis who paid every single country of the assorted 30-odd states contributing to the war—with the reported exception of Canada. While such payments were helpful to the Saudi psyche, rendering the enterprise akin to hired assistance, these payments seriously damaged the finances of the state, the consequences of which are still being felt.

The fact that Saudi Arabia is a land blessed with a precious commodity—oil—leads to a fascinating and enduring myth, that the country is rich and possesses unlimited financial resources, even when the facts belie such perceptions. While Saudi Arabia is certainly comfortable by the standards of developing countries, it is basically a land of modest means. Its economy is smaller than that of Hong Kong's (with Hong Kong's population about a third of that of Saudi Arabia) and its per capita income is about half that of Israel's (a country perceived in need of American financial assistance). It should therefore not be surprising that economic issues are dominant now and may remain so for the foreseeable future.

Largely as a result of the Gulf war and the huge outlays the country had to make (at least $60 billion), Saudi Arabia's national debt is reckoned to be anywhere between 70 and 100 percent of its GDP. Although a good part of the debt involves intragovernmental accounts and very little of it is owed to foreigners, the debt's sheer size and the improbability of trimming it anytime soon acts as a serious constraint on the government's spending abilities. This is crucial for the Saudis, as domestic tranquility and regional stability have been to a large extent ensured through a policy of generous spending. Without this lever, Saudi Arabia's ability to contain regional challenges and domestic disgruntlement is limited, at least so long as traditional Saudi policies are maintained.

That the most serious domestic disturbances since the 1979 Mecca Mosque attack took place in 1994 should not be surprising. In part due to wartime expenditures, the economy went into a recession in that year. In addition, some long-outstanding economic "structural adjustments," which were further exacerbated by wartime decisions to increase subsidies and lower utility tariffs, had to be made, including not only a reversal of such steps but also the imposition of significant increases in fees for utilities and, more importantly, a sharp reduction in agricultural subsidies. All these factors contributed to a marked worsening in the atmosphere of antigovernment agitation within the "fundamentalist" circles that blossomed during the Gulf war that voiced strong objections to the armed American presence on Saudi soil. A crackdown followed and many were jailed. That policy appears to be effective so far.

Domestic economic pressures are compounded by very high rates of population growth. Until fairly recently, Saudi population problems were analyzed along the lines of underpopulation and inadequate human resources. Indeed for a long time the Saudis held population statistics as a closely guarded secret. At one point, when the first national census, taken in the early 1960s, showed a population of only some three million, it was simply rejected. A decade later, the census of 1974 showed a population of seven-plus million, including the expatriate community, which by that time had grown substantially. By 1994, the new census showed the country with more than 17 million, of whom more than 12 million were Saudi. It is thus amusing that the same author who undertook the task of analyzing Saudi demographics in 1982, concluding then that native Saudis were a mere 4.2 million, recently declared that "Mohammed Malthus was alive and well."

The radical change in Saudi demographics is also reflected in changing government employment policies. Until the mid-1980s, because of a lack of sufficient Saudi public servants, all Saudi college graduates were legally obligated to work in the public sector for a period equal to the time they spent in college. The policy was discontinued in 1985. By the early 1990s, Saudi Arabia started for the first time, at least since the oil boom of the early 1970s, to experience "unemployment." It is one of the most challenging problems now facing Saudi decision makers.

Saudi employment issues are atypical. In a country where even college graduates face difficulty finding work, the foreign contingent of the labor force is still *larger* than the native component. Presumably, a version of "import-substitution" policy would provide an easy solution to this difficulty. So far, while the government is acutely aware of the dangers of unemployment, the policies pursued are somewhat incoherent and are no more than an attempt to impose quotas on businesses to ensure that a minimum percentage of Saudis are employed by each Saudi entity, a policy that is both economically inefficient and difficult to enforce. The Saudis recognize that the fundamental problem stems from the fact that access to the Saudi labor market is not restricted, and any employer can always find a foreign worker "cheaper" than a Saudi. To plug this hole in the labor market would require the imposition of taxes, fees, minimum wage legislation, or a combination of all these policies to render the Saudi labor force more competitive. But such action is entwined with the question of taxation, a domestically sensitive issue.

Clearly, even if a restructuring of the labor force were to take place by substituting Saudis for foreign workers, some jobs will always be shunned by the Saudis, and any of these solutions will not be a long—term cure as long as demographic trends do not change in a serious manner and economic growth remains singularly tied to oil prices and production. The challenges facing the decision makers will be further compounded as economic pressures compel women, who now account for only 10 percent of the labor force, to seek employment outside their homes.

On the foreign policy front, Saudi Arabia's position has not substantially changed since the Gulf war. Iraq is a threat and will remain so for at least as long as Saddam Hussein (or his dynasty) remains in power. This problem is manageable for the time being with American commitments to contain the Iraqi leader. Yet doubts linger. For one, there is always the fear that the United States may change its policies due to some calculations, be they domestic or otherwise. More important, a linchpin of the policy of containment is the substantial presence of American troops within Saudi Arabia. This presence, while crucial for the success of containment, comes at a substantial domestic price for the Saudis, and it is doubtful that Saudi public opinion can tolerate this presence indefinitely.

Equally problematic is the relationship with Iran. Although some thawing is currently taking place, Saudi-Iranian relations ever since the revolution of 1979 have been marred by persistent conflict and mutual antipathy. The Iranians wanted to export their revolution and were hostile to most of their neighbors, including Saudi Arabia. The long, bloody war with Iraq contributed to tensions with Saudi Arabia and even led to a limited military engagement. The greatest danger Iran poses for Saudi Arabia, however, probably comes from Iranian attempts to enlist Shiite sympathizers in Saudi Arabia and elsewhere in their anti-Saudi activity. To the extent that reports about an Iranian role in the Al Khobar bombing are accurate, it would constitute the most flagrant hostile act taken by the Iranians since the direct armed conflict during the Iran-Iraq war.

The annual Muslim pilgrimage to Mecca, the hajj, gives the Iranians the opportunity to try to destabilize Saudi Arabia. The Iranians have consistently viewed that rite as a political forum through which political gains could be garnered. By financing huge numbers of Iranian Shiite pilgrims and insisting on their "right" to freely express their politics in Mecca, the Iranians have engaged the Saudis in annual clashes that only served to exacerbate tensions. To contain Iranian hostile activities during the hajj, the Saudis managed to obtain the imprimatur of the majority of Muslim countries for the concept of quota for pilgrims, which caused Iran to stop sending its own for a number of years. In addition to direct action, the Iranians have successfully recruited, at least on one occasion, some Shiite sympathizers who planted bombs in Mecca. Unless a radical change in Tehran takes place, there is no reason to expect these tensions to subside.

The other regional issue posing challenges to Saudi Arabia is the ubiquitous Arab-Israeli conflict. As long as the Palestinians are deprived of their own state, the question of Jerusalem is not settled, and no permanent peace is reached with Syria, the potential for deadly conflict with unpredictable results will hover over the region. There is probably no single issue that so powerfully resonates within Saudi society as the strong feelings held against Israel and its policies. So long as an Arab-Israeli war is avoided, the question of Palestine is generally manageable, but the Saudi government is unlikely to be able to engage in direct relations with Israel short of a final, comprehensive settlement.

Saudi Arabia's other neighbors pose challenges of their own to the Saudi decision makers. The seemingly perennial border problem with Yemen still plagues bilateral relations. Although frequent pronouncements are made about imminent breakthroughs, probably nothing short of a miracle would solve this problem in the short term, mostly because of Yemeni domestic considerations. Be that as it may, it is a problem which is probably manageable at a reasonable cost. The "conflict" with Qatar, while unfortunate in many ways, as Qatar has historically been Saudi Arabia's closest Gulf ally, is more of an irritant than a serious threat. Presumably the border dispute is in the process of being settled, which should help keep the differences between the two countries less disruptive.

The Saudis over the last two decades have been "blessed" with a temporary surplus of oil income, which spared them the agonies of confronting many of the problems typical of "normal" politics and of developing societies. But with a growing and better-educated population, including a strong middle class component, the relatively easy days may be over. Many decisions will have to be taken with respect to the economy and the political structure that have been set aside for a generation now. Tentative steps have been taken, but many difficult political and economic decisions have still to be made. Barring a sudden (and unlikely) oil boom, many of these decisions would entail significant social, economic, and political cost. If the past is any indication, the Saudis should be able to handle these new challenges with reasonable success.

MEMORANDUM FOR THE PRESIDENT

From: Abdulaziz H. Al Fahad

Subject: Critical Strategic Choices in U.S. Policy toward Saudi Arabia

The U.S. Department of State recently released a report, "On United States Policies in Support of Religious Freedom: Focus on Christians." In this report, Saudi Arabia is held to be one of the top transgressors. The country is unflatteringly portrayed as a land where "[f]reedom of religion does not exist," in which "Islam is the official religion, and all citizens must be Muslims." In contrast with other offenders, China for example, which pay lip service to these notions, Saudi Arabia does not even pretend to uphold these liberties and unabashedly declares itself against U.S.-style religious freedoms on Saudi soil. At the same time, this is the only country where the United States is on record avowing to defend it not only in the event of foreign aggression, but also to preserve the existing regime, which so offends the sensibilities of the State Department even against domestic opponents. Such extremes appear to be the natural outcome of marked cultural divergence between the values espoused by the two societies and the convergence of significant interests on the political realm. Tensions between the two elements have characterized U.S.-Saudi relations from their inception and there is no reason to expect them to disappear in the foreseeable future.

Indeed, one of the first encounters between Americans and Saudis took place in the 1920s after King Abd al-'Aziz conquered the Hijaz. Two intrepid U.S. missionaries were determined to spread their notions of salvation in the very cradle of Islam. Caught at the border, they were unceremoniously expelled. Self-confidently but perhaps naïvely, the first "lobby" urging U.S. recognition of the nascent Saudi state were the missionaries of America who hoped to gain better access to the "errant" Arabian souls. Recognition came but Saudi religious policies remained the same.

Originally perceived as part of the British sphere of influence, discovery of oil in the early 1930s in eastern Arabia, where American companies enjoyed monopoly positions, compelled U.S. direct involvement in Saudi Arabia. U.S. policymakers recognized early on the strategic value of the commodity and the huge size of the reserves, describing it as the most valuable prize in human history. The relationship from those days evolved, at times close, at others more distant, but never veering too far from a U.S. commitment, albeit not always explicit, of defending U.S. interests in Arabian oil. The onset of the Cold War further cemented this increasingly close relationship, with the Saudis accepting a U.S. base in Dhahran, to be closed in the early 1960s during the heyday of Arab nationalism.

Even with the closure of the base, the United States still found in the Saudis useful partners against the increasingly radical pretensions of Nasser's Egypt and its supporters. While at that time U.S. concerns for Israel's "security" did not loom large, preoccupation with Soviet influence and communist infiltration ensured that Saudi Arabia would remain a valuable U.S. ally as the Saudis had their own worries about the radical trends of that era. With the rise in global dependence on Gulf oil, Saudi Arabia's importance in the American scheme of things was enhanced. The country, along with the Shah's Iran, was elevated to a "regional influential," which the United States expected to help maintain stability in the Gulf. Even the famous oil embargo of 1973 did not fundamentally harm what was growing into a strategic partnership. With the advent of the revolution in Iran in 1979 and its subsequent war with Iraq, as well as the Soviet invasion of Afghanistan, the United States and Saudi Arabia intensified their cooperation to stem the tide of revolution, war, and invasion.

Largely as a result of those seminal events, matters that were kept in the background had to be brought to the fore. Up until then, U.S. guarantees for the security of Saudi Arabia were understood but not explicitly stated. Fears of the Iranians and the Soviets prompted the United States to develop its rapid deployment force (transformed later into the current "Central Command") to deter outside aggression. Thus was the "Carter doctrine" enunciated in January 1980, declaring the Persian Gulf vital to U.S. interests and explicitly committing the United States to defend, by military means if necessary, the region against any outside attempt to control it. Apparently the doctrine as stated was not sufficient for Carter's successor, Ronald Reagan, who took U.S. commitments to Saudi Arabia even further. In what came to be dubbed as the "Reagan codicil" to the Carter doctrine, President Reagan declared, on October 1, 1981, that the United States "will not permit [Saudi Arabia] to be an Iran." Lest anyone miss the point, this pronouncement was shortly thereafter clarified to mean a commitment on the part of the United States guaranteeing the Saudi form of government against "internal as well as external threats." Thankfully, the "internal" part of the undertaking has not been put to the test.

The biggest challenge for the newly enhanced alliance was the Iraqi invasion of Kuwait. Within three days of the invasion the whole world knew that both countries were explicitly committed to the defense of Saudi Arabia and implicitly to the liberation of Kuwait. The amassing of hundreds of thousands of U.S. troops in Saudi Arabia went as smoothly as could be hoped for and the liberation of Kuwait was accomplished in due course. Apprehensions about permanent, large U.S. presence on Saudi soil were put to rest by the quick withdrawal of the majority of American forces. This military dimension to the relationship is now limited to a small number of U.S. troops involved in the policing of Iraq.

While this strategic relationship has worked rather well, friction is unavoidable. For one, Saudis, with the exception of the Dhahran base episode, have always been reluctant to acquiesce to any peacetime large U.S. military presence in the Kingdom, preferring the "over-the-horizon" option, which shields them from both domestic and regional criticism. While such policy may hamper the defense of the area, it clearly spares the Saudis unwelcome attention. Even the limited U.S. presence dedicated for the containment of Iraq is problematic and the Saudis would prefer to see it disappear as soon as possible.

Other irritants to the strategic relationship include the conspicuous Arab-Israeli conflict. Prior to 1967 and the subsequent heavy U.S. commitment to Israel, the Saudis fulfilled their obligations to their Arab brethren with minimum friction in U.S.-Saudi relations. But once Israel became the preeminent U.S. obsession in the region, noticeable tensions arose corresponding to the ebbs and flows of the Arab-Israeli conflict. Although the Saudis (and other Arab producers) shut down oil production for some time during both the 1956 and 1967 Arab-Israeli wars, only the oil embargo of 1973 assumed Olympian significance (partly due to the changes in oil supply and demand at that time and in North-South relations). The Saudis found themselves in the midst of a maelstrom which did not subside until the lifting of the embargo.

Because of the strong basis for the strategic relationship, even this episode passed without serious damage to the alliance. But an added dimension to this partnership emerged with its own points of friction, namely Saudi attempts to procure U.S. arms which Israel and its domestic supporters were determined to block. The Saudis tried, and even succeeded on occasion, but despite their strategic value to the United States and the cash they were willing to pay, they for the most part had to go elsewhere to shop for their military needs. It was not until the Gulf war that U.S. domestic considerations permitted the Saudis the necessary flexibility to obtain most of their military requirements from U.S. sources.

Paradoxically, it is this latter transformation that has become something of an irritant to the partnership. Among other things, the Gulf war coincided with the end of the Cold War and the reduction in U.S. military procurement. It appears that once domestic objections by Israel and its lobby were mollified, the Saudis became a valued source for funding the troubled U.S. arms industry. The Saudis were now seen as a safety net and they committed, between 1990 and 1995, a reported $62 billion dollars for the purchase of diverse arms and services from the United States at a time when the Saudis had to cut back substantially on their own domestic spending. It is true that the Saudis must have felt a need for some of the purchases; nevertheless a good part of their procurement was more in the nature of "gratitude" for U.S. help during the Gulf war. Thus was born a strange program: foreign aid provided by Saudi Arabia, a small-size economy, to the richest country on earth.

Regional politics still dominates the relationship in many respects. The much-vaunted "dual containment" policy is fraying at the edges in recognition of its if not outright failure, at least limited success. The containment of Iran is felt strongly in the United States, a feeling not necessarily shared by all U.S. allies, including the Saudis. The U.S. policy toward Iran is suspected of being driven in part by lingering resentments over the hostages episode. The Saudis appear to be carefully exploring their own notion of "constructive engagement," a policy that other Gulf states, notably Oman and Qatar, have pursued. All this, however, is clouded by the yet-uncertain responsibility for the bombing of U.S. military barracks in Al Khobar last year. So far the Saudis and the Americans have been equivocal about Iranian involvement. Should it be determined that Iran had a role in the incident, pressure will mount to retaliate, the nature of which may be disagreed upon by the two allies. There is fear of a U.S. strike that, while therapeutic, may simply drive Iran into more radicalism, with unpredictable consequences.

In contrast to Iran, containment of Iraq appears to be working smoothly. There is of course always bewilderment in Saudi Arabia over some U.S. decisions, as when the United States is offered clear provocation only to retaliate in what is perceived in the area as meek ways. Barring some dramatic development in Iraq, this policy seems destined to continue. The Saudis are thus assured of their own security and, simultaneously, along with other oil producers, of the opportunity to share in the windfall resulting from the embargo placed on Iraqi oil exports.

There are other points of concord and discord between the two countries. On the positive side, Saudi Arabia is a firm believer in free enterprise (even before it became fashionable). The country offers the United States a relatively affluent market and the latter ranks first among Saudi Arabia's trading partners. The Saudis have adopted policies strongly favorable to U.S. companies, which enjoy some noticeable advantages and maintain significant presence in the Kingdom.

Yet for all their solicitousness towards the United States, the Saudis have not shied away from confronting the Americans when they thought it was in their best interest. The clearest example is the long-running disagreement over the Arab-Israeli issue. In addition, the Saudis have also procured types of weapons which the United States wished Israel to monopolize. The best known incident is Saudi purchase of strategic missiles from China in the mid-1980s. Partially as a result of American heavy-handedness, the Saudis were compelled to declare the U.S. ambassador at that time persona non grata.

For its part, the United States has made it a ritual to criticize Saudi Arabia in its annual human rights report, which invariably paints an unfavorable picture of the country. All perceived Saudi transgressions are expounded at length. They are chastised for lack of free speech, censorship of the press, lack of elections, religious intolerance, curtailment of women's rights, mistreatment of expatriate workers, and even capital punishment. Taken at face value, the State Department seems to approve of little in the country.

These declared differences, however, may be just as helpful for the alliance. The Americans can point to their "unwavering" commitment to human rights and their willingness to scold even close allies. But it is the Saudis who probably benefit the most. For in its censure of Saudi Arabia, the United States is confirming indirectly Saudi independence and that Saudia Arabia is not an American "puppet." This stems from the fact that many of the issues for which the Saudis are routinely reprimanded are matters of general consensus in the country. As the recent State Department report attests, Americans criticize the Saudis for actions (or lack thereof) on things in respect of which the Saudis have little or no flexibility. It is inconceivable that Saudi Arabia would or could change its religious policies; hence censure in this regard can be safely ignored. Even the much-discussed issue of women's rights is problematic for the Saudis as it is the populace in general, and not necessarily the government, which is the "culprit." Ignoring, or even defying, American entreaties in this respect enhances the legitimacy of the Saudi government in the eyes of its own citizens.

In many ways, the United States has an easy task. In contrast with many other societies, the United States in its dealing with the Saudis is spared the difficulty of choosing between support of its values or of the governing elite. To the extent there is any domestic disapproval of the Saudi government, it comes from the fringe of radical Islamism whose espoused values are anathema to Americans. Perhaps predictably, when the *New Yorker* magazine saw fit to have a long, sympathetic piece about one of the leading Saudi dissidents, it was none other than the *New Republic* which came to the Saudi government's defense.

In addition, America knows nothing of the place and its ways and appears to be aware of its own limitations with respect to "engineering" other alien societies. This ensures that U.S. conflicts with Saudi Arabia over human rights are reduced to an annual ritual which both sides manage to take lightly. It should therefore not be surprising to expect little change in the relationship. It is premised on a community of interests rooted in oil and geopolitics. Both countries value stability and abhor revisionism. Both oppose the spread of destabilizing radical Islamism. And both recognize the incompatible elements of their social, political, and religious outlooks. The marriage of convenience should last for as long as the underlying interests demand it, just another striking example how politics indeed make strange bedfellows.

MEMORANDUM FOR THE PRESIDENT

From: Robert Satloff

Subject: Critical Strategic Choices in U.S. Policy toward
         Saudi Arabia

Every day, the United States reaffirms a set of "critical strategic choices" about Saudi Arabia and about issues that affect our relationship with Saudi Arabia and our view of the kingdom. Thinking about future U.S. decisions must begin with those decisions that are tacitly made on a daily basis.

Choice (Ongoing): *That a stable, friendly Saudi Arabia is vital to the security of the United States and merits the extension of a U.S. military guarantee against external threats.*

The case for this "strategic choice" is less obvious than it seems. Among countries the United States is pledged to protect, none is more unlike the United States than Saudi Arabia. On sociocultural grounds, the two societies are on opposite ends of the spectrum on such items as democracy and personal and group freedoms (e.g., speech, association, religion, assembly). Politically, the two countries have less in common today than in the past, when the Saudis were staunch allies in the Cold War. Saudi "moderation" on regional political issues is, of course, relative—the kingdom participated in the ostracism of Egypt after Camp David, has been decidedly unenthusiastic about the regional component of the Madrid peace process (the multilateral track), and has only been episodically constructive (and even then in a peculiarly Saudi-like, behind-the-scenes way) in support of the Oslo process and Jordan-Israel peace. Economically, Saudi Arabia may be the world's leading oil producer and home to the world's largest oil reserves, but in the era of free markets, that happenstance of geology may not be as important as it once was. After all, less than 10 percent of the oil consumed in the United States comes from Saudi Arabia; of imports, which constitute approximately 50 percent of U.S. oil consumption, Saudi Arabia is not the leading source—indeed, nearly half of oil imports are from the Western Hemisphere (Venezuela, Canada, and Mexico) with Saudi

Arabia providing less than one-fifth.[1] Should U.S. and Western investment in the Caspian and other new or comparatively untapped sources prove successful, Saudi Arabia's relative importance to U.S. (and Western) interests will decrease further.

Nevertheless, the United States has chosen to regard the defense of the kingdom of Saudi Arabia as a vital national interest. This apparently reflects an assessment that: (1) the current management of Saudi Arabia helps to advance wider U.S. interests than any of its alternatives; (2) support for the current management is likely to ensure continuity of the Saudi approach to relations with the United States; (3) continuity will become more important when reliance on Saudi oil resources grows in the future (as forecast by the U.S. Department of Energy). Each component of that assessment *itself* reflects a "critical strategic choice" regarding Saudi Arabia.

Choice (Ongoing): *That the best strategy for the defense of the Gulf—and, hence, Saudi Arabia—is a policy of reliance on the forward presence of U.S. land- and sea-based forces to fill the vacuum caused by the absence of any powerful, moderate stabilizing country in the region (i.e., "dual containment").*

One cannot address the tactical and operational problems that the United States may face in Saudi Arabia and in relations with the Saudi regime—e.g., defense against terrorists targeting U.S. troops—without reassessing the strategic arena in the Gulf.

"Dual containment" is the most recent U.S. strategy to secure America's core interest in the Gulf: to ensure unhindered access to the region's oil (half the world's proven reserves) and gas (one-third the world's proven reserves). From 1972 to 1979, the United States relied on the "twin pillars" of Iran and Saudi Arabia to ensure regional stability; this policy collapsed with the fall of the Shah. From 1980 to 1990, U.S. policy was to build up Saudi defenses, nurture incipient defense cooperation among the countries of the Gulf Cooperation Council, and most importantly, adopt a "balance of power" approach toward the two other regional powers, Ba'thist Iraq and Islamist Iran; this policy collapsed with the Iraqi invasion of Kuwait, which underscored the fact that both Iraq and Iran advance policies fundamentally inimical to U.S. interests and that Arab Gulf countries themselves are woefully incapable of providing for their own defense against external aggression. The elements of a new strategy, designed to fill the vacuum opened by the absence of any moderate power in the Gulf, were implemented by the Bush administration in the wake of Desert Storm. The Clinton administration inherited this de facto strategy of containing Iraq and Iran, named it "dual containment," and via the increased and sustained deployment of U.S. troops in the Gulf and the imposition of an economic embargo on the Tehran regime, applied it more broadly than did its predecessor.

Like previous Gulf security strategies, the objective of dual containment is to prevent any disruption of oil or gas supplies, to promote the stability of those friendly regional states who help provide access to energy resources, and to deter any unfriendly country, ideology, or movement from exercising control over the region's energy resources.[2] It does so by recognizing the absence of any friendly power in the Gulf able to assert leadership and project force in a moderate, pro-Western direction; while Saudi Arabia may (or may not) have the will, it certainly lacks the ability. Dual containment recognizes the sad reality about Iraq and Iran, seeks to contain their aggressive policies, bolsters inter-Arab cooperative security efforts and, most importantly, brings U.S. military force into the region in an unprecedented way as the counterbalance that preserves Gulf stability.

In practice, to the extent that dual containment was designed to minimize the ability of Iraq and Iran to threaten immediate U.S. interests in the Gulf, this strategy has registered some success. Saddam Hussein has been kept "in a box," deprived of much of his air space, his weapons of mass destruction, his ability to import in order to rebuild his army, and the regional political influence that comes with military power. Likewise, Iran has been denied its previous access to international investment and credits and has been forced to curtail spending on its conventional military buildup.

However, from the beginning, the longer-term goal of dual containment was to compel the regimes in Iraq and Iran to change their behavior. By this measure, U.S. policy has not succeeded. Iran and Iraq continue to engage in aggressive policies—especially the use of terrorism and the pursuit of weapons of mass destruction—that threaten regional stability and vital U.S. interests. Moreover, there have been a series of indications that the United States is finding it increasingly difficult to sustain even current levels of pressure against either Iraq or Iran. Iraqi resistance to the work of the UN Special Commission, the body charged with destroying Iraq's weapons of mass destruction, is growing; at the same time, the willingness of key states to use military means, if necessary, to support UNSCOM is visibly waning. The 1998 crisis over UNSCOM inspections reinforces this pessimism. The Iraqi opposition is in disarray; many regional states are considering a decision to reach an accommodation with Saddam; and the Iraqi armed forces are stronger now than at any time since the end of the Gulf War (though, of course, much, much weaker than they were before 1990). On the other side of the Gulf, there is still no viable opposition to the Iranian regime despite erosion of popular support for clerical rule; the Iranian military has focused its limited acquisition budget on weapons systems that pose potent new threats to Gulf security, like submarines, as well as on the two ends of the confrontation spectrum—terrorism and acquisition of weapons of mass destruction; and the United States has been unable to persuade our European or Asian allies to join our economic embargo against Iran.

As a result, U.S. efforts to maintain (let alone tighten) containment of these two regimes has grown increasingly unilateral, and less compelling to the Iraqis and Iranians. This is reflected in deep differences between the United States and many of its Gulf War allies (both European and Middle Eastern) on key aspects of containment strategy. These differences became painfully apparent during the inspections crisis of early 1998. This is also reflected in the unprecedented expansion of a U.S. military ground presence in the historically closed societies of Arab states in the Gulf. One unwelcome side effect of this U.S. presence is the growth of popular resentment against the United States and its local allies, upon which terrorists have already sought to capitalize via attacks against U.S. installations in Riyadh (November 1995) and Dhahran (June 1996). This has created the paradoxical situation in which U.S. forces are protecting themselves against terrorism from *within* countries they are there to defend as they protect those same countries from external adversaries.

The key choice U.S. leaders routinely reaffirm is the decision to maintain the policy of dual containment as the main effort to promote political change that would reduce the threat to U.S. regional interests and, when either Iraq or Iran adequately moderates its behavior, eventually to redeploy U.S. troops off Gulf soil. Other policies, such as sustained military operations or clandestine initiatives, have been considered or even attempted (as in the northern Iraq-CIA debacle) but are not now the centerpiece of U.S. policy. As a result, the U.S. has essentially adopted a waiting-game approach, on the assumption that the U.S. position in the Gulf (as well as the will and ability of Gulf allies, especially Saudi Arabia) can sustain this policy until political change in Iraq or Iran renders it unnecessary. Inter alia, this reflects a certain static assessment of Saudi threat perceptions (domestic versus external, Iraq versus Iran) and Saudi strategy toward addressing those threats that constitutes a set of key strategic decisions that are tacitly (and continually) reaffirmed.

Choice (Imminent): *Whether—and how—to retaliate for Iranian complicity in the Al Khobar bombing.*

Like others, this decision focuses on U.S. policy elsewhere in the Gulf but has direct implications for Saudi Arabia and U.S.-Saudi relations. While President Clinton has vowed to respond appropriately should Iran be found culpable in the Al Khobar bombing, which killed 19 U.S. servicemen, the issue is not of law but of politics, policy, and strategy; political decisions, not legal standards, will be the yardstick by which one judges culpability. From the start, this decision was complicated by the mixed signals emitted by Riyadh. Saudi officials have suggested that renegade Saudi Shiites were responsible—a charge which is eminently possible but which also has the effect of diverting internal and international attention from a potentially more serious problem of disaffection (and terrorism) from within the majority Sunni population. However, a Shiite link raises the prospect of Iranian complicity, and considerable circumstantial evidence apparently does exist which implicates Iranians in "preblast" contact with some of the alleged perpetrators and in providing "postblast" safe haven to some others. This raises the stakes from a domestic crisis to a potential regional confrontation, though the Saudis themselves would never retaliate militarily against Iran nor would they, by themselves, seek UN support for international sanctions against Iran. (Notably, the Germans did not pursue the UN course when the proof of Iranian complicity was irrefutable.) In March 1998 the Saudi government announced that its investigation was complete—no suspects were named. A public report was promised—eventually.

For the United States, the issue is more complicated: Should the United States opt for a UN response? If that fails, should the United States opt for a military response? The Saudi approach to the investigation complicates the problem. It is hard to imagine any U.S. military action unless Saudi authorities publicly agree in any American identification of the "culprits."

The surprise election of a relative social moderate in Iran's presidential election has further complicated the issue. In this context, numerous parties, Saudis, Israelis, and others, have warned against military retaliation but for different reasons.[3] Many Americans and others seeking some form of rapprochement with an Iranian regime they view as a fixture on the regional landscape consider the issue of terrorism as little more than an irritant that should not be allowed to interfere in a strategic shift in relations with Iran.[4] In contrast, those Israelis who have cautioned against military retaliation have done so out of a belief that popular discontent inside Iran is so strong and pervasive that it would be shortsighted to give the mullahs an excuse to fan the flames of Persian nationalism so soon before the Islamic house of cards crumbles from within.[5] Throughout, Saudi Arabia has sent mixed signals, at times highlighting the reputed Shiite origins of the terrorists, at other times sending high-ranking emissaries to Tehran to warm relations. It is difficult to discern whether those diplomatic missions are designed to convince Washington not to attack Iran, to convince Iran not to retaliate against Saudi Arabia, or both.

Choice (Future): *To what extent, if any, should the United States seek to secure its own long-term interests in Saudi Arabia by emphasizing the need for economic and/or political reform in our private and/or public relationship with the kingdom?*

Among U.S. policymakers, analysts and scholars, there is general recognition of the breakdown of the grand bargain that has been the lubricant of Saudi stability for a quarter century—i.e., too little money to guarantee the continued loyalty of too many people. However, observers disagree on two issues: how imminent this threat may be to Saudi stability, and what, if anything, the United States ought to do about it.

The latter question is particularly complex because it could entail stark policy trade-offs. For example, most U.S. allies in Saudi Arabia's economic situation would receive a stern lecture from Washington and international financial institutions about the need to cut subsidies, trim imports, rationalize government spending, and otherwise implement market reforms. However, urging Saudi Arabia to pursue this path, especially in the absence of political reforms that might cushion the socioeconomic impact of economic retrenchment, is only likely to aggravate domestic discontent with the rule of the Al Saud. At the same time, it is likely to cost the United States a not inconsequential share of its export market to Saudi Arabia, which is one of the United States's largest markets, having purchased more than $40 billion in U.S. goods since the Gulf War (including arms).[6] Similarly, advising the Saudis to make their government more participatory as a way to defuse discontent (one hesitates to use the term "democratize"), in line with the Clinton administration's first-term strategy of "democratic enlargement," runs the risk of alienating Saudi leaders and inter alia emboldening precisely those elements in society that are most inimical to U.S. interests, the Islamist radicals. Yet, as both ends of Pennsylvania Avenue focus their attention on issues of human rights (including, for example, a new emphasis on religious freedom), maintaining the Saudi "exemption" from this sort of scrutiny will be more difficult to maintain.

Ironically, the difficulty posed by this "friendly tyrant" conundrum *is likely to grow* once the threat from either Iraq or Iran decreases and some from of balance-of-power strategy emerges to replace dual containment. That is because a balance-of-power strategy presupposes the reintegration of either Iraq or Iran into the international community, with full participation in the oil market and a more neutral status in the calculus of Gulf security. In that circumstance, Saudi Arabia will become *relatively* less important to U.S. interests, lowering the barriers that economic reformers and political critics now face in addressing Saudi issues directly.

Choice (Future): *When Abdullah becomes king, how seriously, if at all, should the United States view departures from the pro-American "Fahd model" of Saudi policy?*

The choice Washington makes on the preceding issue is likely to be influenced by its view of the policies pursued by Saudi leaders, especially Crown Prince Abdullah. Once Abdullah accedes to the throne, it is to be expected that he would seek to leave his own imprint on Saudi policy, especially on issues of relatively secondary strategic significance; however, at a certain point, accumulated departures from Fahd's precedent even on lesser issues would amount to a strategic deviation (or at least will be viewed as such by numerous outside observers). For example, while the "pro-American" Fahd and the "Arab nationalist" Abdullah almost surely hold similar views on the core element of Saudi external security—reliance on a U.S. security guarantee—their reputed differences on a range of other issues (from the Arab-Israeli peace process to a possible rapprochement with Iran) could overshadow the degree of continuity. Those differences will surely be amplified by the contrast between one prince viewed as a relative moderate for more than 30 years and another who enters office with a reputation for having originally opposed the U.S. deployment in 1990 and with a family link (by marriage) to Syrian leader Hafez al-Assad.

This issue could be aggravated by the all-too-common phenomenon of a ruler seeking to alleviate domestic discontent by an appeal to nationalism (or, perhaps in this case, to religio-nationalism). It is not difficult to imagine a scenario in which Saudi rhetoric (and even some Saudi actions) on inter-Arab and inter-Islamic issues grows more strident, as the kingdom grapples with a worsening economic crisis, rising popular dissatisfaction, and even the emergence of a more widespread radical (probably Islamist) political opposition. Into this mix one might add efforts by the Saudis to acquire sophisticated weaponry (including ballistic missiles) from non-American and even non-Western sources.

A Saudi Arabia that pursues a more neutralist agenda could raise a series of sensitive policy choices for the United States. For example, in this situation, would Washington respond to the acquisition of Chinese ballistic missiles by an Abdullah-led government as mildly as it did to the Fahd-led government? Or, if an Abdullah-led government reimposed the secondary and tertiary aspects of the Arab boycott of Israel or actively supported an Arab League suspension of all normalization efforts with Israel (as threatened in a recent League resolution), would Washington be less reticent to engage in a public critique of Saudi economic or social policy? In this general set of circumstances, divining U.S. choices regarding Saudi Arabia will certainly be much more difficult than they are today. (They will look much more like the 1970s, but the contrast with the 1980s/1990s will make the decisions more complicated.)

Nonchoice: *Selecting the next Saudi monarch (and his successor)*.

While Washington faces a set of sensitive policy choices regarding Saudi Arabia, one variable in the Saudi political equation that the United States cannot affect (and probably should not try to) is succession. In recent years, Washington's record in forecasting leadership change has been fairly poor (e.g., Israel, May 1996; Iran, May 1997). Actual efforts to bring about desired change have not been more successful, and when they were they required an enormous investment of U.S. political, military, or other capital (e.g., Haiti). In Saudi Arabia the personality of the supreme leader is important, but given the consensual nature of strategic decision making, it is relatively less important than in many other countries. When the famously closed nature of the Al Saud is factored into the equation, it makes sense to conclude that trying to influence the succession process inside Saudi Arabia is likely to be counterproductive. This is one decision that U.S. officials are likely to learn about from CNN.

ENDNOTES

1   International Energy Agency, *Statistics: Oil, Gas, and Electricity,* 1996.

2   In this regard, it is important to recall that the danger of a regional hegemon is not only that it could restrict the flow of oil and gas, but that it could, through coercion, restore discipline to the oil cartel and thereby control the supply and price of energy as a political and economic weapon against the West. Moreover, the danger of an adversarial country exerting hegemony over the region's oil resources—as the Iraq case bears out—also includes what that country can do with the vast income it would earn: namely, fund aggressive programs of conventional rearmament and nonconventional weapons development that would be used as tools of political and ideological expansionism and strategic challenge to wider U.S. interests.

3   To be more precise, many have suggested using a purely legal yardstick for determining guilt, which would effectively rule out retaliation since no case against Iran is likely to be strong enough to stand up under the equivalent of judicial scrutiny.

4   Former Ambassador to Saudi Arabia Richard W. Murphy, for example, has referred to the al Khobar investigation as a "stumbling block" in the effort to build "improved relations with Tehran." See "It's Time to Reconsider the Shunning of Iran," *Washington Post,* 20 July 1997.

5   See the address by Uri Lubrani, Israel's coordinator of activities in southern Lebanon and former envoy to Iran, to The Washington Institute, 15 May 1997.

6   One side effect of the loss of a substantial piece of this export market may be decreased willingness of the United States to bear a disproportionate burden for the cost of Gulf security relative to our allies. Statistics compiled from Department of Commerce reports, June 1997.

MEMORANDUM FOR THE PRESIDENT

From: Your Staff

**Subject: Summary of Discussion on America and Saudi
        Arabia**

This is our summary. It may not necessarily reflect everyone's views, and some may disagree with the conclusions.

1. The long-standing U.S.-Saudi relationship was founded on oil. That foundation remains durable. Though we are skeptical about estimates of energy supply and demand, the available evidence indicates that oil from Persian Gulf will be even more important during the next decade, if not beyond. Saudi Arabia will continue to play a nearly unique role in being able to moderate prices and rapidly increase production in a crisis.

2. The U.S.-Saudi relationship is also based on shared strategic interests. While Saudia Arabia funds extremist groups, it also tries to be, and is widely seen as, a more moderate counter to the Iranian example of Islamic politics within the Muslim world. Saudi Arabia has also, on occasion, been an important force for regional political stability and progress toward Arab-Israeli peace.

U.S.-Saudi relations exhibit a longevity, and a depth of business and cultural relationships, that could eventually build a more intangible basis for friendship. Obstacles include the inward-looking tendencies of publics in both countries, as well as the profound differences between the conservative Muslim society of Saudi Arabia and the society and culture of the United States.

3. The Saudi-American (and Gulf Cooperation Council) coalition against Iraq is under strain. An American force presence in the region at or near the current scale of activity seems necessary for the immediately foreseeable future. The possibility of moving U.S. Air Force activities out of Saudi territory should and will be considered on grounds of cost, domestic politics in both countries, the forces needed to police the no-fly zone over southern Iraq, and the distraction of pro-

tecting ground installations against terrorist threats. Further, the presence relies on prepositioned military equipment in Kuwait and Qatar, as well as Saudi Arabia, a point which highlights the importance of inter-Arab cooperation if the coalition is to be sustained.

4. The Saudi-American partnership may be less vulnerable to arguments arising from the Arab-Israeli peace process than to disagreements arising from divergent policies toward Iran. Therefore it will be crucial to work with the Saudi government in devising appropriate policies toward Iran in the period ahead.

5. The United States should take an active interest in the domestic governance of Saudi Arabia. The operational objectives of such an interest should include much better evaluation of information about the circumstances of the Kingdom. The United States should be careful not to overreact to reports or gossip about Saudi succession politics within the royal family. The Saudi government has been more stable and resilient than many observers, for decades, have thought would be the case. The United States should not distance itself from the royal family or pressure for specific changes in the Kingdom's political processes. The Saudi government's ability to liberalize its society is probably constrained less by governmental attitudes than by the conservatism in the society, a major obstacle to reform-minded ministers.

6. Saudi Arabia is not a rich country, by many standard measures. Lower government revenues could strain the social bargain that supports the government. Friendly economic advice might be welcomed, but the structural recommendations will require hard political choices. The United States might help the Kingdom understand those choices and what is at stake, but the political calculations and policy judgments can only be made by the Saudis.

Questions: Will there be a greater demand for political participation, and how will the ruling family deal with it? Is political extremism increasing in Saudi Arabia? If so, is it likely to threaten the government?

AMERICA AND IRAN

MEMORANDUM FOR THE PRESIDENT

From: Your Staff

Subject: Questions for Discussion on America and Iran

1. How serious are the threats posed to America by Iran?

    *   Overt aggression or subversion of Iran's neighbors

    *   International terrorism against Iran's enemies (and Americans)

    *   Development of weapons of mass destruction

    *   Hostility to the Arab-Israeli peace process

    *   Hostility to development of the Caspian Basin

2. Is current U.S. policy, centered on diplomatic and economic isolation of Iran using unilateral economic sanctions, both sufficiently effective and sustainable?

    *   Is there a basic clash between U.S. foreign policy and U.S. energy policy? If so, how should priorities be set?

    *   How should U.S. policy define success?

    *   What are the consequences of policy for other relationships and policy goals of the United States?

3. Are more effective and sustainable alternatives available to U.S. leaders?

    A. Dialogue

    *   What would the United States offer or expect in such discussions? Estimate of success?

    *   How would such an initiative interact with domestic politics within the United States or Iran, or their relationships with their allies?

    B. Firmer confrontation

    *   Is the security posture of the United States and its allies adequate to counter the spectrum of Iranian threats (immediate case: Al Khobar)?

- Can the diplomatic and economic isolation of Iran be made more effective?

C. Should a new policy combine elements of both A and B?

MEMORANDUM FOR THE PRESIDENT

From: Judith Miller

**Subject: What about Iran Should (or Shouldn't)
          Concern You**

Before answering *this* question, we should ask another: What should the United States *know* about Iran? First, Washington should recognize that the revolution it has been confronting in its tragicomic way for some 18 years has long been over. Yes, in typical fashion, the heirs of the revolution still control the guns. And yes, Iran continues to conduct and abet international terrorism and encourage instability throughout the world. And yes, almost predictably, Iran has tried to compensate for its failure in so many practical endeavors by accelerating its pursuit of weapons of mass destruction. And finally, yes, Iran is trying to undermine American efforts to make peace between the Arabs and Israel and foster greater openness and stability in the Middle East—perhaps America's strongest objection to the militant Islamic regime. But despite the persistence of such outrages (which may or may not include complicity in the bombing of the Khobar Towers apartment complex in Dhahran, Saudi Arabia, in which 19 American soldiers died), the radical fervor that once posed an expansionist threat to the region, terrifying Iran's neighbors and the West alike, seems to have abated.

When and how the revolutionary passion ebbed says much about the nature of the Islamic system today and what may be Washington's limited ability to encourage Iran to mend its dangerous ways and transform itself from what the Clinton administration calls an "outlaw state" into a more or less "normal" country.

Scholars still debate precisely when, if not why, the revolution began sputtering out. According to Edward Shirley, the former CIA analyst whose brilliant new memoir captures both Langley's incompetence as well as the irresistible dynamism and infuriating duality of Iranian society, the end came on February 16, 1990, with a spontaneous, two-hour riot not against hunger or war but against the cancellation of a soccer match at the Amjadieh Stadium only a few hundred yards from the former American embassy where U.S. diplomats were held hostage in 1979 and 1980 by those intent on preventing any an Iranian-American rapprochement.[1] After hearing that the match had been canceled, Shirley writes, the disappointed fans stormed through the streets of Tehran shouting "Down with Rafsanjani!" the then supposedly moderate president, and more provocatively, "Long live the Taj," the prerevolutionary name of a soccer team, which also means "the crown" in Persian.

The outburst by the angry young men of the slums that had supplied a disproportionate share of Tehran's volunteers in the devastating eight-year war that Iraq had initiated shocked Iran's mullahs and forced them to conclude that the mustazafin, or the "disinherited," the once obedient, faithful poor in whose name the revolution was made, were fed up with the revolution's failed promises, exhausted by the eight-year war with Iraq, and infuriated by the government's growing corruption. A terrifying thought took hold among the mullahs: the foot soldiers of the revolution might no longer be loyal to the clergy.

The soccer protest was small stuff, however, compared to the violence that subsequently engulfed the squatter slums of cities throughout the country. By 1991, the rioting reached Mashhad, the gateway to Central Asia. The city, Shirley writes, is the site of the shrine of Imam Reza (d. 817), the eighth of the twelve Imams who form the historical and mystical inspiration behind Twelver Shi'ism, the scorned, defeated, minority branch of Islam—which is nonetheless the primary Islamic sect of Iran, Iraq, and Lebanon. But here in this revered pilgrimage city, the formerly faithful burned down a large part of their town, including the Islamic Cultural Center.

Others argue that Iran's radical faith gave out even earlier. Roy P. Mottahedeh, Harvard's leading Persia watcher, and Daniel Brumberg, of Georgetown University, trace the revolution's demise to the 1989 revision of the constitution by former President Ali-Akbar Rafsanjani.[2] The constitutional reforms not only undercut clerical rule, they also began to distance "church," or in this case, mosque, from state.

Still others date the historical turning point to the bitter speech earlier that year by the Ayatollah Ruhollah Khomeini, the self-styled "armed imam" without whose charismatic leadership there might never have been an Islamic revolution. At Rafsanjani's urging, Khomeini had reluctantly agreed to "drink poison" and end the war with Iraq (which he could have ended in 1982) rather than permit the debilitating conflict to destroy his revolution and his country.[3]

Khomeini had issued another extraordinary decree that same year, a ruling critical to appreciating the Islamic revolution's evolution. Appearing to equate the survival of his own government with that of Islam itself, a belief that fostered on his part ever greater pragmatism, if not moderation, Khomeini declared: "Our government has priority over all Islamic tenets, even over prayer, fasting, and the pilgrimage to Mecca." In other words, the interests of the state, the political incarnation of Islam on earth, took precedence over those of the religion. If the interests of Iran meant buying weapons from the "Great Satan" to fight Iraq, so be it. If they dictated destroying a mosque, it was leveled.

The implications were as stunning a departure from traditional Shiite doctrine as the creation of his own God-sanctioned leadership post— the "Walayat al-faqih," the country's supreme leader, who would rule on earth with God's authority until the return of the twelfth Imam, whose reappearance on earth as the messiah would usher in judgment day. Acceptance of this radical notion of a preeminent jurist who would rule before the messiah's return and whom all Muslims would be religiously bound to obey was not an easy sell, but by arresting or neutralizing the grand ayatollahs, the most influential Islamic clerics, a majority of whom opposed his theory, the Imam Khomeini, the revolution's glowering killjoy saint and ever astute politician, got away with it.

By Khomeini's death in 1989, however, few doubted that revolutionary enthusiasm had waned. Khomeini had embodied the revolution's sense of Islamic universality—its Iranian-led, pan-Islamic revolutionary mission. But even the Imam himself, the so-called "hope of the world's disinherited," the "standard bearer" of revolutionary Islam, had undermined Islam's universal mission towards the end of his rule and sacrificed for what cynics might call raisons d'etat Iran's obligation to adhere strictly to traditional religious mores and values and to support

Islamic movements abroad. While the revolution's proclaimed commitment to revolutionary Islamic universalism would be espoused by the next Supreme Guide, it would endure mainly as rhetoric, and at that, when strategically advantageous to Iran. Khomeini, in fact, would have no real successor.

While Iran continued killing its enemies at home and abroad and fomenting terror and instability, the revolution internally entered a new phase, or "a new order," as then Foreign Minister Ali Akbar Velayati bluntly told some 250 Western, Asian, and Arab oil officials who met in the ancient imperial city of Isfahan at the end of the Gulf war in 1991. When it came to economics, the revolution was over. Iran had to rebuild, to dig itself out of debt, Velayati told the assembled oilmen.[4]

Iran's new order, or what one Arab commentator calls the "second republic," marked the rise to power of, and subsequent power struggle between, President Rafsanjani, the clerical son of wealthy pistachio farmers and merchants, and Ayatollah Ali Khamenei, the unimpressive cleric whom other senior clerics had chosen as Iran's new supreme guide.[5] (Khamenei was reportedly promoted expediently from the lesser rank of hojatolislam, or "authority on Islam," the day Khomeini died.) While Iranian revolutionary politics in Iran had always been factionalized, without the unassailable Khomeini to adjudicate competition among the clerical power centers intensified, making decisions on matters other than those involving national security far more difficult and time-consuming, inconsistent, and often blatantly contradictory. Iran became ever more of what one analyst called a "factionocracy."[6]

At the same time, Iran appeared begrudgingly to recognize the limits of its regional power and the folly of openly confronting the United States militarily. While some Western officials predicted in 1991 that Iran would not sit idly by while an American-led coalition bombed neighboring Muslim Baghdad, Iran did just that. It stayed on the war's edges, quietly providing intelligence about Iraqi movements to Kuwait and savoring America's bashing of its historic rival. And even when Iraq bombed the holy Shiite shrines in Najaf and Karbala and massacred Iraqi Shiites who had revolted against Saddam Hussein at America's prompting after the war, there was only a peep of protest from the

Iranian clergy and no response at all from the Islamic government in Tehran. And Rafsanjani was bitterly disappointed, Iranian officials say, when, having heard George Bush's inaugural promise that "Good will breeds good will," Iran helped free American hostages in Beirut and got virtually nothing for its efforts.

Exporting revolution and relegating Iraq and the rich Gulf sheikdoms to the "dustbin of history," as Imam Khomeini had vowed, were downplayed in the revolution's second phase. The particular form of Shiite political fervor being peddled by non-Arab, Shiite Islam had few takers among Iran's Sunni Arab neighbors. Under Rafsanjani, Tehran gradually began developing mostly cordial ties with the previously despised Gulf states. Iran's new leaders opted for a quieter—and some analysts argue more dangerous—military buildup in the Gulf, a "shop 'til you drop" campaign to buy nuclear technology and other weapons of mass destruction, and often fingerprintless terror (in Buenos Aires and perhaps in Riyadh and Dhahran, Saudi Arabia, as well). But once again, ambition outstripped both resources and competence. Iran was unable to spend about half the $10 billion allocated to military schemes between 1989 and 1994, even before the United States had fully implemented its "dual containment policy" and concomitant sanctions. And the embarrassment of the Mykonos case, in which a German court last April blamed Iran's top political leadership, including the ostensibly pragmatic President Rafsanjani, for the murder of Kurdish dissidents in a restaurant by that name, led to the temporary suspension of Europe's efforts to improve Iranian behavior through "constructive dialogue."

Internally, the government grew ever more aware of the need for economic reform. By 1995, per capita income in real terms had fallen to roughly a quarter of what it was before the revolution, and population growth, though no longer spiraling out of control, continued to outstrip economic expansion. But again, brave talk of privatization and reform by Rafsanjani's technocrats succumbed to political reality: Iran's hardliners, aligned in ever-shifting, opportunistic coalitions with the country's *bunyods* (the 15 or so officially nongovernment foundations whose spending is not reflected in published budgets and which are said to control as much as 30 percent of Iran's wealth) and the *bazaari* (the traditional class of merchants and moneylenders who resisted free trade and a more rational economic order), blocked real reform. Iran weathered the dangerous debt crisis of 1993-1994, but inflation, high unemployment, and stagnation continued.

While Iranians still endured waves of harassment and repression at the hands of Hezbollah (radical thugs sanctioned by the security services), the government effectively also shelved Khomeini's dream of creating "homo Islamicus," a new Shiite man committed to spreading the rule of Islam throughout the world and shunning the traditional Persian taste for sensual pleasures.[7]

Islamic fervor was also supplanted by resurgent Persian nationalism. This hallmark of the new order was really an expression of traditional nationalism with an Islamic vocabulary. Increasingly, Iran's Persian-ness has run deeper than its Islam whenever the two collide.

Now with the election of Sayyid Mohammad Khatami by almost 70 percent of the electorate, men and women over the age of 15—10 million more of whom voted in this contest than the last one—the Iranian revolution seems to have entered yet another stage. This "third repub-lic," says the same Arab commentator who christened its predecessor, reflects the unmistakable disenchantment of an overwhelming majori-ty of Iran's more than 65 million people not only with the ruling gov-ernment, but more broadly, with clerical rule in general, and some say, with Islam itself.

Few observers predicted 18 years ago that the effect of Khomeini's rev-olution might be to alienate Iranians from their religion, half of whom were not even born when the revolution occurred. But then almost nobody—Western or Iranian—predicted Khatami's stunning victory, either.

While young Iranians remain grateful to Khomeini and his revolution for getting rid of America's repressive, autocratic puppet, the Shah, and giving them a sense of national independence, the overwhelming rejec-tion of the establishment clergy's candidate, Ali Akbar Nategh-Nouri, the parliamentary speaker, by Iranian voters (young and female voters, in particular) can only be seen as a devastating indictment of, and

protest against, the ruling clergy and what they must consider an ominous disgust with what passes for "Islamic" government in Iran today.

This new, deeper level of discontent became vividly clear during my
last visit in late 1995 when my young translator resisted visiting
Isfahan, the fabled home of classical Islam's most stunning architec-
ture. When I asked Nazila, who like most young, middle-class Iranians
favors officially forbidden and omnipresent blue jeans, lipstick, and
American films and music, why she had cringed when I suggested visiting Isfahan, she shrugged and replied, "Who wants to see a place with
so many mosques?"

Some clerics have eloquently articulated their anxiety about young
Iran's growing alienation from Islam in action, concern that has
prompted a few brave souls even to urge the clergy to abandon politics
and return to their classrooms in Qum for the sake of their faith. But no
one gives up power voluntarily. And Khatami, for all his seeming
strengths, is very much a product of the Iranian system.

Nevertheless, his electoral landslide gives him more potential clout and
hence opportunities for reform than that enjoyed by his predecessor.
Rafsanjani's 1993 election drew 63 percent of possible voters to the
polls; Khatami attracted a 91 percent turnout. Plus, he also drew support from groups on opposite ends of the political spectrum: from the
leftist Coalition of the Imam's Line, which favors continued state control of the economy and a more equal distribution of wealth, to most
members of the pro-Rafsanjani Servants of Construction, which opposes state economic control and favors increased foreign investment and
improved relations with the West. America and Great Satan-bashing
moved few voters in the most recent contest: "the economy, stupid,"
coupled with demands for greater personal freedom were the campaign's most compelling themes.

In addition, Khatami is taking over after Iran has weathered the worst
of the economic restructuring required by the Gulf war. So he is inher-
iting a system with a slightly larger private sector and relatively
stronger economy than what Rafsanjani found when he took over in
1989.[8]

Supreme Leader Khamenei may well have top billing and the guns, but for the moment, Khatami has the people. And recalling Tehran's soccer riots and Iran's politically active and volatile population, Khamenei, a shrewd cleric and experienced politician, might hesitate to openly obstruct the reforms Khatami has promised and which appear to command such popular support.

But given Iran's well-entrenched power centers with so much at stake, the third stage of Iran's disintegrating revolution might well mean even greater tension and power struggles, as well as continuing foreign policy stalemates and economic stagnation. The number of powerful players, if anything, may be expanding, rather than consolidating. In March the Council on Determining the Expediency of the Regime was given greater powers under its new head, former President Rafsanjani. While it is usually assumed that the former president will remain supportive of his supposed protégé, he could well decide to carve out his own, more independent role and power base by shifting support between Khamenei and Khatami.

Finally, there is the issue of Khatami's real intentions. Is he really— dare we use the word after Washington's repeatedly embarrassing searches for enlightened Islamist leaders—a moderate? Even if he is, will he be able to resuscitate a failing system? If he is moderate and can reform the system, is it in America's interests for him to succeed? Given the revolution's historical evolution outlined above, these, along with Tehran's outlaw activities, are the issues that should concern Washington.

In the months since his election, we have learned much about Khatami, the 55-year old hojatolislam whose impeccable religious credentials are reinforced in the eyes of many Iranians by his status as a descendant of the Prophet. The son of Ayatollah Ruhollah Khatami, much respected for his scholarship and piety, Mohammad Khatami was a former student of Ayatollah Ali Montazeri, the cleric who resigned under pressure as Khomeini's deputy and heir apparent in 1989 and a force for moderation in domestic, if not foreign policy. (Montazeri, who remains effectively confined to Qum, still has the most popular class in Qum with about 1,000 students, says Roy Mottahedeh.)[9] Fluent in at least three languages, Khatami has a master's degree in philosophy from Tehran University. Though he was a founding member of the hardline Combatant Clerics Society, friends and associates describe him as open-minded, tolerant, and, in some matters, liberal.

In his decade-long tenure as minister of Islamic guidance, he introduced bold reforms in Iran's cultural policies, among them, the lifting of the ban on chess, music, and an independent press. He is also credited with having helped revive Iranian cinema and promote independent civil groups and associations. Forced out of his post by radicals in 1992—ostensibly for permitting a female singer to be broadcast on radio—he became the head of Iran's national library, where he wrote at least two books, portions of one of which have recently been translated and are now available in a single volume in English intended to highlight his relatively enlightened outlook, views that Iran specialists call highly unorthodox among the ruling clergy.

His scorn for religious dogmatism, for example, is eloquently articulated in *Hope and Challenge, The Iranian President Speaks*.[10] While the first two chapters contain by now ritualistic denunciations of Western society for its imperialism, neocolonialism, and desire for cultural hegemony and warn against "any form of reconciliation and appeasement," they also caution against confronting the West through violence or military struggle. "We must confront the thought of the opponent through reliance on rationality and enlightenment," he writes, "and by offering more powerful and compelling counter arguments," phrasing which implicitly endorses, if not open dialogue, contacts and a calm exchange of views.

Khatami also finds much to admire in the West, and not just its science and technology. "We have to keep in mind that Western civilization rests on the idea of 'liberty' or 'freedom,'" the most cherished values of all mankind, he says. "To be fair, [the West] has successfully cast aside the deification of regressive thinking that had been imposed on the masses in the name of religion," and has "broken down subjugation to autocratic rule," all of which he calls "positive steps."

Rejecting the notion of a clash of civilizations, he argues that like its Western counterpart, Iranian society, too, faces a deep-seated crisis stemming from unrealistic expectations and "discord within" generated by "secular intellectuals" and "unenlightened, religious dogmatists." He clearly concludes that the greater threat comes from the "dogmatic believers," who in the name of Islam, and projecting "the aura of religious legitimacy," seek an anachronistic "return" to a vanished Islamic golden age by trampling religious and intellectual freedom. "When confronting the enemy in the name of rejecting the West and defending religion, if we step on freedom, we will have caused a great catastrophe," he concludes.

Alternating in true revolutionary form between contradictory expressions of confidence in Islam's cultural superiority and an almost paranoid sense of encirclement and beleaguerment, Khatami argues that a new, improved Islamic society can emerge only "if we have the ability to absorb the positive aspects of Western civilization, and the wisdom to recognize the negative aspects of it and refrain from absorbing them."

While it is usually foolhardy to assume that politicians in opposition mean what they say and write or will actually implement their pledges once in power (consider, for instance, the encomiums to democracy contained in the early works of Sudan's de facto autocratic leader, Hassan al-Turabi) Khatami's tenure as guidance minister justifies at least some optimism about his intentions.[11]

Khatami, by contrast, has said relatively little in his essays and books or during the campaign about foreign policy, traditionally the domain of the supreme guide. But his new 23-member, all-male cabinet—his lone female vice president for environmental affairs does not need parliamentary approval—places pragmatists in several key posts, including the ministry of intelligence, traditionally responsible for killing dissidents at home and abroad, and the minister of Islamic Guidance, his own previous post.

But obstacles to real reform abound. And Khatami, who lacks even close to a majority in the conservative parliament, will have to maneuver among the country's competing power centers and factions far more adroitly than his supposedly pragmatic predecessor did. To succeed, he will have to prove not only more creative, but a tougher and more skilled politician than Rafsanjani, who, while sporadically raising

Western hopes, failed to make the country productive, prosperous, or predictable.

Furthermore, securing greater social and cultural freedom for Iranians at home, at the price of tolerating continued bad behavior abroad and continued pursuit of weapons of mass destruction, may soften internal opposition to the regime—but it is not likely to win Iran the international confidence needed to attract investment capital and spur acceptable levels of growth.

Is it in America's interest for Khatami to succeed? Probably yes, depending on how one defines success. Some argue that Khatami's "reforms" may spell the de facto end of Iran's repressive Islamic autocracy. But simply enabling the regime to survive in a more efficient form with equally and possibly even more menacing capabilities could hardly be considered an achievement by the West.

Some want Khatami to fail because they oppose religiously based governments on grounds that Islamic orders, by their nature, will fail to offer citizens real political and economic freedom or to guarantee women and minorities equal standing and full civil and human rights; such systems are also likely to be pugnacious in international affairs, the argument goes. But while religious governments tend to be autocratic, they need not be inherently anti-Western—consider Oman and Saudi Arabia, for instance. And as this paper has argued, Iran's repressive, anti-Western, Islamic government has already undergone so many stunning and subtle shifts, withstood so many changes, and rationalized away so many internal contradictions to adjust to different political circumstances, it might be premature to discount the possibility that Iran could further evolve into an "Islamic" system mainly in name only.

Moreover, most analysts see no likely promising alternatives to the current regime in Tehran. Most Iranians loathe the socialist Islamic group the Mujahideen-e Khalq—the Khmer Rouge of Islamic militants—which has terrorized the Islamic Republic for years from its base in enemy Iraq. Though popular with Congress and with lavish offices in Washington, the Mujahideen would probably be neither democratic nor pro-Western if they seized power in the wake of riots and the collapse of the current Islamic order. Another occasionally mentioned alternative, the young son of the late Shah, also enjoys little support. Thus, in the short run, the triumph of Iran's radicals, or chaos and unpredictable change, seem the main alternative to Mohammad Khatami's stated desire to create a kinder, gentler, more efficient Islamic state.

ENDNOTES

1   Edward Shirley, *Know Thine Enemy, A Spy's Journey into Revolutionary Iran* (New York: Farrar, Straus and Giroux, 1997), 23. (Shirley is a pseudonym.)

2   Roy Mottahedeh, interview with author, and Daniel Brumberg, *Spokesmen for the Despised,* (Chicago: University of Chicago Press, 1997), 17.

3   Farhad Kazameh, "The Iranian Enigma," *Current History,* January 1997.

4   Elaine Sciolino, *The New York Times,* 2 June 1991.

5   Asaad Al-Hayat Haidar, quoted in *Mideast Mirror,* 23 July 1997.

6   Bahman Baktiari, "Khatami's Presidency: The Beginning of a New Era?" unpublished manuscript, 25 July 1997.

7   Safa Halari, Interview by *Iran Monitor,* 23 July 1997.

8   Bijan Khajehpour-Khouei, "Iran's Presidential Election: A New Phase in Post-Revolutionary Development," The Council on Foreign Relations, *Muslim Politics Report,* May/June 1997.

9   Roy P. Mottahedeh, "Shi'ite Political Thought and the Destiny of the Iranian Republic," in *Iran and the Gulf: A Search for Stability.* Jamal. S. Al-Suwaidi (Abu Dhabi: The Emirates Center for Strategic Studies and Research), 1997.

10 Published by Binghamton University and Brigham Young University, and translated by Alidad Malfinezam.

11 Judith Miller, "Global Islamic Awakening or Sudanese Nightmare?" cited in Brumberg.

MEMORANDUM FOR THE PRESIDENT

From: Shaul Bakhash
Subject: How Iranian Leaders View America and
         the World

Ever since they made a revolution and seized power 18 years ago, Iran's clerical leaders have considered themselves to be engaged in a unique undertaking to create an exemplary Islamic state based on Islamic law and superior to both communism and capitalism. "We should be a model to the world," Ali-Akbar Hashemi-Rafsanjani, Iran's president until 1997, said some years ago. "We should be able to present Islam as an alternate model for human society."[1] According to the former chief of the judiciary, Abdol-Karim Musavi-Ardabili, such is the uniqueness of the Iranian experiment that the establishment of a true Islamic state has not been attempted for 14 centuries, not since the Prophet established his exemplary community in seventh-century Arabia. Momentous consequences ride on the outcome of the Iranian enterprise. The eyes of the entire world, Musavi-Ardabili has said, are on Iran. According to Iran's former president and present supreme leader, Ali Khamenei, "failure for the Islamic Republic means failure for Islam."[2]

If the Islamic Republic is yet to realize the ideal society based on Islamic law and social justice, in the official Iranian view, it is well on its way; and the Iranian revolution, in any case, has already proved itself. It overthrew a corrupt, autocratic regime, restored religion to its rightful place in society, stood up to and humiliated the United States, and fought off an aggressor, Iraq, supported by the great powers of both East and West. More recently it has successfully fought off an American policy of sanctions designed to isolate and impoverish it. The Iranian revolution is living proof that Islam is the preeminent weapon for the world's exploited peoples to use against the exploiters and is thus a paradigm for revolutions elsewhere in the Islamic and Third World. "Our revolution," Khomeini said several years ago, "is not tied to Iran. The Iranian people's revolution was the starting point for the great revolution of the Islamic world."

Since the overthrow of the monarchy, Iran's leaders have anticipated, hoped for, and connived at the establishment of Islamic regimes outside Iran's borders. In the first year of the revolution, Iran's first president, Bani-Sadr, predicted that the conservative, "reactionary" regimes in Saudi Arabia and the Persian Gulf emirates would be swept away by revolutions similar to Iran's. Khomeini prosecuted Iran's war with Iraq for many years after Iraqi troops had been expelled from Iranian soil not only to punish Saddam Hussein but also to see an Islamic regime established at Baghdad, a development, he believed, that would force other Persian Gulf states to follow suit. Iran, for many years, expected its Shiite Hezbollah protégés and the rising Islamic tide to triumph in Lebanon—until Mohammad Hussein Fadlallah and other Lebanese Shiite clerical leaders persuaded Iran that an Islamic state was not yet a viable blueprint for Lebanon's multiconfessional society.

Islam, Iran's leaders continue to assert, is the wave of the future. In an oft-repeated formula, the senior living Shiite cleric in Iran remarked in 1991 that "the vacuum that has been created with the disintegration of communism . . . and the vacuum that will be created in the near future when, God willing, capitalism will be overthrown, should be filled by Islam."[3]

Iran's leaders have claimed a universal significance not only for their revolution; they have also claimed a kind of universal spiritual leadership for the architect of that revolution, Ayatollah Khomeini, and now for his successor, Ayatollah Khamenei. Iran's clerics spoke of Khomeini as leader not only of Iran's Shiites, but of Shiites everywhere; not only of Shiites but of the worldwide Islamic community. "Today, the Imam [Khomeini] has regency over 50 million Muslims," another senior cleric, Ayatollah Ali Meshgini, said a year before Khomeini's death. "Tomorrow, God willing, he will rule over one billion Muslims." President Rafsanjani reported on return from an official visit to the Soviet Union shortly after Khomeini's death, that in the Caucasus, even Soviet Muslims wept when he mentioned Khomeini's name. "The hope of the world's disinherited" was one of the many honorifics by which Khomeini was addressed.

Khomeini took his role as spiritual leader and spokesman for the Muslim world with utmost seriousness; his words and actions implied a transnational authority, or at least a transnational Islamic responsibility, extending beyond Iran's borders. In January 1989, for example, Khomeini addressed a message to Mikhail Gorbachev, applauding the Soviet leader for abandoning the false God of communism, urging him to avoid the equally false God of capitalism, and advising him to return to God, read the Koran, and study the Islamic mystics and philosophers.[4] Iranian commentators made explicit the startling historical precedent implicit in this offer of guidance to the misguided. Legend has it that in the seventh century, the Prophet sent a similar message of warning, and a similar invitation to follow the straight path, to the rulers of two great regional empires, Iran and Byzantium.

Again, it was as the defender of the world Muslim community against the supposed insults and blasphemous content of the novel *The Satanic Verses* that Khomeini condemned Salman Rushdie to death. Khomeini addressed his last will and testament not only to the people of Iran but "to all the Muslim nations and the oppressed of the world." Each year, Khomeini encouraged Iranian pilgrims making the annual hajj to Mecca to participate in demonstrations to "disavow the infidel"—that is, to disavow the United States and the great powers—and invited pilgrims of other nations to do the same. This great ingathering of Muslims, he insisted, had a political as well as a religious purpose: to unite Muslims against the "world-devouring" great powers and against autocratic, irreligious Muslim rulers at home. Almost every year until the bloody clashes between demonstrators and Saudi police in 1987 caused Iran to change tack, his slogan-shouting followers helped foment clashes between the Iranian pilgrims and Saudi authorities in Mecca and Medina.[5]

Khomeini and his lieutenants felt little compunction in publicly denouncing other Muslim heads of state, arguing it was an Islamic duty to denounce the tyrant, the corrupt leader who had strayed from the Islamic path. In his last will and testament, a document intended as a guide on policy to his successors, and which was solemnly unsealed and publicly read after his death, Khomeini described King Hussein of Jordan as a "criminal peddler," and King Hassan of Morocco, and President Mubarak of Egypt as American lackeys and associates of the "criminal Israel." He called for public cursing of the rulers of Saudi Arabia for their alleged "treachery" against the house of God.[6]

Khomeini's successor, Ali Khamenei, has aspired to a similar role as spokesman for the world Islamic community. He sees himself as Khomeini's heir and seeks to capture for himself the prestige and authority he believes Khomeini enjoyed among Muslims worldwide. He wishes to bolster his position, which is far weaker than Khomeini's, with constituencies at home.[7] He aspires to a major role for Iran on the international stage. He speaks out of a conviction that the Islamic world must unite and gird itself for struggle with an exploitative, threatening West.

In the last few years, Khamenei has thus championed the cause of Muslims in Bosnia, denounced the death, allegedly at American or Western hands, of Muslims in Somalia and Iraq, and supported the cause of the Islamic regime in Sudan. At every opportunity, he denounces America's alleged quest for worldwide hegemony and its appetite for other people's resources. He has insisted that Khomeini's death sentence against Salman Rushdie stands and that it is incumbent on Muslims to carry it out. He has adopted an uncompromisingly hostile attitude to the Arab-Israeli peace talks, arguing that the Palestinian question and the ultimate disposition of Jerusalem is "an Islamic matter" on which presumably all Muslims, not just the Palestinians, must have a say.[8]

This universalistic streak in Iran's revolutionary ideology impels Iran's leaders to support Islamic movements, and to project the Iranian revolution, outside Iran's borders. They do so out of both conviction and calculation. First, if Iran is the preeminent Islamic state, then it must be *seen* to be championing Islamic causes. The support that Iran lends, by word or deed, to Islamic movements in Iraq or Lebanon, in Sudan or the West Bank, is thus a token of its Islamic credentials. In 1994, Iran began to supply arms and financial assistance to Bosnia's hard-pressed Muslims; and financial aid to the Bosnian government has continued.

Second, the political base of the regime is narrow. Most Iranians have not been involved in the political process and probably find the regime's unrelenting anti-Western rhetoric mind-numbing, its claims to an endless string of stunning successes at home and abroad unpersuasive. But identification with Islamic causes helps the regime silence radical clerics and factions within the ruling group who are ready to label the least sign of accommodation with the West an abandonment of revolutionary principles; and it appeals—or so the regime imagines—to its hard-core supporters in the Revolutionary Guards and revolutionary committees, a segment of the clergy, Islamic associations in the universities, the influential lobbies of the families of revolutionary "martyrs" and war veterans, and so forth. It was to this constituency that the leader of the conservative and politically powerful Association of Combatant Clerics was appealing during the 1996 parliamentary elections when he accused a rival political group of technocrats associated with the more pragmatic policies of President Rafsanjani of wishing to resume ties with the United States, end Iranian opposition to the Arab-Israeli peace process and the "Zionist regime," and lift the death sentence against Salman Rushdie.[9]

Third, Iran's leaders view themselves as competing for the hearts and minds of Muslims worldwide against various rival claimants: the "corrupting" attractions of Western culture, secularists of all stripes, other activist Islamic states like Saudi Arabia. They imagine that a militant stance on Islamic issues enhances Iran's standing with Muslim communities beyond Iran's borders. Fourth, by bolstering Islamic regimes, or helping propel like-minded Islamic opposition movements to power, the Islamic Republic believes it will enhance its own security and render more hospitable the regional and international environment in which it operates. Demonstrably, the Islamic card, coupled with other forms of assistance, has yielded dividends—for example, allowing Iran to become a player in the internal politics of Lebanon and securing it a presence in Bosnia.

Finally, the support Iran provides to Islamic movements and causes outside Iran's borders also has nuisance value; it provides Iran with leverage against the United States and other countries whose policies it finds incongenial. In a way, the Iranians seem to be saying: If the United States treats Iran as an international pariah, imposes sanctions and prevents American companies from doing business with Iran; seeks to persuade and pressure its trading partners to deny Iran credits, technology, and arms; excludes Iran from Persian Gulf security arrangements and Caspian Sea oil deals, threatens Iran by its military presence in the Gulf region; and makes an issue of Iran's human rights record, then Iran can make life in the region difficult for the United States. It can act as spoiler in the Arab-Israeli peace process, depict the United States as the enemy of Muslims, support movements—for example, Hamas and Islamic jihad on the West Bank—inimical to U.S. interests. Iran's Islamic activism predates but is in part also a response to a U.S. policy of "containment," to Iran's perpetual fear, its perpetual sense of impending encirclement.

Again, if Egypt cooperates with the United States or aspires to a military presence in the Persian Gulf, then Iran can make life uncomfortable for President Mubarak by supporting the Islamic regime in Sudan. If Iran fears—as it does—that peace between the Arabs and the Israelis will permit Israel to establish diplomatic relations and trade with the Persian Gulf states and challenge Iran's economic, military, and diplomatic ambitions in the Gulf, then Iran will encourage its Hezbollah protégés to attack Israeli positions in southern Lebanon and try to wreck the peace process. The United States wishes to exclude Iran from regional and international councils; but Iran, having earned credits with Bosnia's Muslim leaders, shows it is a player in world affairs.

Implicit in the worldview of Iran's leaders, or at least the worldview they attempt to project to their own countrymen, is a Manichaean sense of the universe, in which the forces of Islam are locked in desperate battle with the exploitative great powers. Khomeini's last will and testament dwells at length on the "Satanic objectives" of the superpowers. They are intent on "toppling Islam," plundering Iran and exploiting its resources, he wrote. They have hatched a plot to undermine Iran's religious and national identity and culture; to cause Muslims to lose faith in Islam and to alienate them from the clergy; to inculcate in youth a secular ideology and a misplaced admiration for Western values. For this purpose they infiltrated the schools and universities, government organizations, and even the clergy; and they placed the graduates of an alien educational system in key positions in Islamic states. Most of the present-day rulers of Islamic countries, he wrote, are lackeys of these "world-devourers."[10]

Khomeini's successor as supreme leader, Ali Khamenei, articulates a similar view. For 200 years, he has said in a variety of forums and in numerous variations on the same theme, corrupt and puppet governments have permitted colonial regimes to dominate Muslim states, alienating Muslims from their heritage and values and inculcating in them a Western culture of corruption and permissiveness—and all this to facilitate the plunder of the material and human resources of the Muslim lands by Western interests.[11] In 1993, Khamenei led a renewed campaign against the so-called Western "cultural assault" against Iran.

The campaign ostensibly aimed at a cleansing films, plays, art, and literature of corrupt Western values, reviving a culture of Islamic authenticity, and ensuring that women, whose hairlines seemed to be stealthily advancing from beneath their scarves, observed proper Islamic dress. The campaign was in part a reflection of the struggle, born of the revolution, between the Westernized intelligentsia, on the one hand, and, on the other, of both the traditionalists and the revolutionary newcomers to the cultural scene, whose cause Khamenei was championing. It was time, Khamenei said, to give the true sons and daughters of the revolution—as opposed to Western-influenced intellectuals who allegedly dominated the cultural institutions—a role in making films and directing plays, and greater opportunity to have their artwork displayed, their books published, and their plays performed. The campaign against the Western "cultural onslaught" was also a convenient means of silencing demands for greater freedom of speech and press, an opening up of the political system, and a less confrontational attitude toward the West.

According to Iran's leaders, the West and the East (meaning the old, Soviet-bloc "East") fear Islam, are hostile to it, and wish to destroy it because it threatens an agelong Western hegemony over Muslim lands. Iran has been singled out as the target of American and great-power animosity precisely because it is the preeminent Islamic state. Iran is the "voice," the "standard bearer" of Islam.[13] It is the "vanguard Islamic nation." It is the champion of the world's deprived and oppressed masses, both Islamic and non-Islamic.[13] It has taken upon itself the burden of leading the resistance to the "shameful" Arab-Israel peace accords. It is a model that others will emulate and the pole around which one billion Muslims will unite. It thus threatens the whole system of Western or great-power domination. "Which Islamic country is the most vigilant . . . and most fearless against arrogance?" Khamenei rhetorically asks. The obvious answer: "Islamic Iran." "All the hostilities in the world," he has said, "are, first and foremost, aimed against us."[14]

As Iran's leaders look from the perspective of Tehran at the post-Cold War world, a sense of triumphalism is curiously intertwined with a sense of defeatism and despair. On the one hand, the Islamic tide seems irreversible. The Islamic movement triumphed in Iran; the Hezbollah are major players in Lebanon; an Islamic state has been established in Sudan. An Islamic political party came to office in Turkey and was eased out only through pressure from the military. Only tanks and Western perfidy prevented the Islamic movement from coming to power in Algeria. If the PLO-Israeli accords constitute a "treachery" to the Palestinian cause, it is nevertheless the Islamic uprising on the West Bank that forced Israeli backs to the wall, and the Islamic movement that will render the peace accords irrelevant. Regimes in Egypt, Tunisia, and other Muslim states are under pressure from their Islamic opposition.

President Rafsanjani reported after a visit to Senegal and Sudan in December 1991 that the triumph of the Iranian revolution was everywhere evident. The admiration for Iran among the poor even in remote Senegalese towns was "astounding."[15] In Sudan crowds of impoverished but enthusiastic admirers held aloft pictures of Khomeini that they had torn out of old newspapers, and waved Iranian flags they had fashioned out scraps of cloth. "The people of Sudan were imitating you," he told Iranians on his return. "They were openly saying . . . the revolution of Iran is our model . . . They were saying that the Imam [the Iranian leader] is also their leader."[16]

On the other hand, Iran's leaders look around and seem to see nothing but doom and gloom. The collapse of the Soviet Union resulted in a unipolar world, with the United States, which is bent on world domination, as the only superpower. The United States used the Gulf war substantially to reinforce its presence in the Persian Gulf; and Kuwait,

Saudi Arabia, and other Gulf emirates abjectly acquiesce in the American domination of the region. One billion Muslims and a host of Muslim states lack unity and do not play a role commensurate with their numbers in major world decisions. Nothing, in the Iranian view, better illustrates the weakness of Muslims and the subjugation of Arab rulers to America's will than the PLO-Israeli peace accords. Muslims simply came to the negotiating table, Iran's leaders repeat, and signed away the rights of a whole nation.

When Ayatollah Musavi-Ardabili surveyed the state of Muslims around the world following the Gulf war, he found that everywhere Muslims were in difficulty. Whether in Somalia, Afghanistan, Kashmir, Palestine, Lebanon, or Iraq, Muslims were facing tribulation and death, yet were helpless to act, even seemed indifferent to their condition. "O you one billion Muslims," he asked, "what has happened to your Islamic zeal? What has happened to your Islamic courage?'[17] And, speaking of the PLO-Israeli accords, Khamenei echoed him: "Why should the world of Islam be so weak and in need of others? Why must the world of Islam beg from its enemies? . . . Why should the Islamic nation be in such a sorry state? . . . Why don't the Islamic governments especially some Arab governments wake up?[18]

What, then, is to be done? In advancing its ideological and "Islamic" goals, Iran has utilized different strategies. It has cooperated, where possible, with other like-minded governments. But Syria and Sudan (and, in earlier years, Libya) aside, such governments have been few and far between. In one country, Lebanon, Iran has assiduously and carefully built up an effective network of allies and structures of support—clerics beholden to Iran, armed contingents drawing on Iranian support, and mosques, religious seminaries, schools, clinics, and other social service organizations important to the local Shiite community and dependent on Iranian funding. In Bosnia, it is attempting to replicate the Lebanese achievement, albeit on a smaller scale and in less favorable circumstance. However, for a variety of reasons, these remain exceptional cases.

Iran has also gone over the heads of governments to direct its appeal at Muslim communities in general or to work with opposition Islamic movements in particular. Musavi-Ardabili, speaking in the aftermath of the PLO-Israeli accords, concluded that nothing can be expected from the governments of Islamic states: "Governments are mercenaries. Governments are puppets," he said. "Hoping that governments will resist Israel, resist the United States—there is not a one per cent probability of that. There is only one thing—and that is the nations. Whenever [the great powers] confronted the people, they were defeated."[19]

The Islamic Republic claims, of course, that it "exports" the revolution only through teaching and example, not by interference in the internal affairs of other countries. In fact, it has utilized not only teaching and example, but also a variety of other means, including supply of money and arms, hostage-taking, terrorism, and-in the case of Iranian dissidents abroad—assassination, to advance its policy aims. (Some senior clerics, admittedly not at the time in office, advocated even more direct action. As a response to the PLO-Israeli accords, Musavi-Ardabili proposed that Muslims form "resistance cells" and attack U.S. interests everywhere, so that Americans "do not even dare to go to the bathroom, or buy a sandwich from the market and eat it, for fear of being poisoned.") But Iran's leaders continue to place a great deal of emphasis on the power of the word, on propaganda, on encouraging Islamic movements, on arousing peoples, in their aspiration for a coalescing of Islamic forces in a powerful tide against the United States and Iran's other rivals and enemies.

Obviously, Iran's foreign policy is not dictated by ideology, in the terms I have defined it here, alone. As I have pointed out elsewhere,[20] Iran's foreign policy is characterized by a strong strain of pragmatism as well. The rhetoric of Islamic triumphalism and hostility to the West is often manufactured primarily for domestic consumption. Ali Akbar Velayati, who, until he was replaced in 1997, had been Iran's foreign minister for well over a decade, was hardly an ideologue. His successor, Kamal Kharrazi, was for many years Iranian ambassador to the UN and had a reputation of desiring an accommodation with the West. A radical rhetoric often masks, or coincides with, hard-nosed foreign policy objectives. Iran's unbending opposition to the Arab-Israeli peace process conveniently reinforces support for its Hezbollah protégés in

Lebanon; and Iranian support for Hezbollah happens to serve the purposes of Iran's close ally, Syria. But the rhetoric tells us something of the regime's self-image. Because it subsists side-by-side with the imperatives of a more pragmatic foreign policy, it helps delegitimize or at least undercut the government's desire for normal traffic with the community of nations. Iran's foreign policy is best understood as the result of a dialectic, or a tension, between ideological and pragmatic considerations. This tension helps explain the often contradictory nature of foreign policy. The relative strength of ideology and pragmatism tends to wax and wane, depending on domestic and international factors, personalities, and the nature of the issue involved. Most often, Iran's foreign policy seems to run on parallel tracks: it is both ideological and pragmatic in temper, both revisionist and status quo-preserving in intent.

This duality was dramatically reflected during 8th summit of the Organization of the Islamic Conference (OIC) in Tehran in December 1997. Iran's supreme leader, Ayatollah Khamenei, inaugurated the conference with a speech which echoed several of the themes described in this essay. He accused the United States of "global arrogance" and a desire for world domination and called for withdrawal of American forces from the Persian Gulf, which he described as "an Islamic sea." He spoke about the threat to Islam by a Western materialist culture rooted in "money, gluttony and carnal desires." He criticized the nefarious influence of the "global Zionist media," denounced "the Zionist regime" in Israel as "hegemonstic, racist, aggressive and violent," and described the Arab-Israeli peace process as "unjust, arrogant, contemptuous and finally illogical." On behalf of "55 Islamic countries and one billion and several million people," he demanded a permanent seat for Muslim states on the UN Security Council.

By contrast, Iran's new president, Mohammad Khatami, called for a dialogue between the Islamic world and the West and urged on Muslims "the judicious acquisition of the positive accomplishments of the Western civil society." The Muslim world, he said, could move forward only by utilizing "the scientific, technological and social accomplishments of Western civilization."[21] Iran used its position as proud host of the OIC summit both to reinforce its claim to speak for the Islamic world and also to reach out to neighboring Islamic states, including several, like Saudi Arabia and Egypt, which it had denounced as reactionary and American lackeys in the past.

Iran's foreign policy practitioners have also managed to "quarantine" some areas of foreign policy from the dictates of the radical rhetoric Iran's leaders articulate. Iran, one might say, has followed a policy of "selective radicalism" in the pursuit of its foreign policy goals. Iran's confrontational style in foreign policy applies to some areas and countries, and to some issues, but not to others. For example, Iran maintains a highly confrontational posture toward the United States. But it has not allowed this to affect its relations with Japan and the countries of Western Europe. Relations with these countries are generally tolerable and, in the economic sphere, sizable. In 1993, Japan, Germany, Austria, and Italy, among others, agreed to reschedule Iran's short- and medium-term debts, providing significant relief for Iran's strained balance-of-payments position. Despite its rhetoric, Iran is not engaged in a perpetual war with the West. On the contrary, as a counterweight to the United States, it has consciously and successfully cultivated the other military and industrial powers, including Germany, France, China, Japan, and Russia. It is often also resourceful and flexible; denied access to weapons and nuclear technology in Western Europe, Iran has turned to Russia, China, and North Korea. The Islamic Republic dealt with the "Great Satan" and bought arms from Israel during the Irangate affair. Syria remains a close ally, although President Assad has dealt harshly with his own Islamic Brotherhood.

Nearer home, although friction seems endemic in Iran's relations with Saudi Arabia, Iran has nevertheless managed to maintain tolerable relations with Riyadh and the Gulf emirates as well. Iran fulminates against the American presence in the Persian Gulf, but its criticism of Kuwait for the basing agreement it signed with the United States has been muted. Its unrelenting opposition to Israel notwithstanding, Iran maintains excellent relations with Oman and Qatar, two Arab states that have recognized Israel.

Like the Shah's government, Iran under the Islamic Republic attaches primary importance to stability along its borders, and in advancing militant Islamic causes, it distinguishes between what we might call the "near abroad" and the "far abroad," between countries neighboring Iran and those that lie at a greater distance. Iran's relations with Pakistan, and India, are good. It has not tried to stir things up in the newly independent Muslim republics in the Caucasus and Central Asia. Iran stood on the sidelines in the civil war in Tajikistan in which 20,000 to 50,000 people—largely Muslims—lost their lives; and the government gives many indications that it prefers a continued Russian presence in the Caucasus and Central Asia as a stabilizing force.

The improvement in Iran's relations with Turkey began long before the Islamic Welfare Party came to power in Istanbul in 1996. Iran likes to cast itself in the role of peacemaker among Muslims and between Muslims and their neighbors. At one time or another, it has tried to mediate disputes between the warring factions in Afghanistan and Tajikistan, the rival Kurdish parties in Iraq, the governments of Azerbaijan and Armenia, and even between the emir of Bahrain and his Shiite subjects. Iran's Islamic activism seems, today, to be reserved more for countries farther away rather than for immediate neighbors: for Lebanon, the West Bank, Sudan, Bosnia.

Besides, while much is made in Washington of Iran's armaments programs, Iran's sense that it lives in a dangerous neighborhood is not entirely fanciful. Instability is endemic along Iran's borders with Afghanistan and Azerbaijan and, potentially, in Central Asia as well. Iraq remains a threatening and unpredictable neighbor. The potential breakup of Iraq, at which the Iranians sometimes think the United States is conniving, fills Iran's leaders with dread. The United States itself is a powerful and menacing military presence. The arms purchases of Saudi Arabia and other Gulf states far exceed those of Iran.

The 1997 presidential elections suggest there is strong aspiration, certainly among the general public and even among some in the leadership, for "normalcy" in foreign policy. Khatami was elected by a landslide in May 1997, in large part because he campaigned on a platform of respect for freedoms, the rule of law, and civil society at home and, implicitly, moderation abroad. His election has strengthened the inclination to build bridges to neighboring states and in Europe. Since taking office, Khatami has gone out of his way to reassure the Gulf Arabs of Iran's peaceful intentions. His call for a "constructive dialogue" with the United States appeared sufficiently persuasive to elicit a positive response from Washington. But the pragmatists are not yet in control, and the ideological component of foreign policy remains strongly in evidence.[22] Its principal themes have been consistent since the revolution: a belief in both the uniqueness and the worldwide relevance, especially to Muslims, of the Iranian revolution; a belief in the revolution's exportability; a deep hostility to the United States; a conviction that the United States is itself deeply hostile to the Islamic revolution; a conviction also that certain aspects of Western culture are threatening to Iran's national and Islamic identity, to its very being; an inclination toward cultural and religious assertiveness to counter this threat; a fear of "encirclement" by a coalition of unfriendly outside powers; a proud sense of Iran's own regional and international weight and worth, and a demand that the international community take cognizance of Iran's importance; an inclination to appeal over the heads of governments to the hearts and minds of Muslims outside Iran's borders; as in the case of Pan-Arabism and its aspiration for Arab unity, an aspiration for an Islamic unity and a hope for the eventual triumph of the Islamic cause in a hostile international environment (a goal which perpetually eludes Iran's leaders but which they continue to pursue because it appears to remain perpetually within reach).

These ideas do not dictate, but they help shape, Iran's foreign policy. They represent the convictions of one faction in Iran's ruling coalition whose influence and fortunes shift, but whose weight continues to be felt. These ideas fuel a rhetoric which Iran's leaders routinely propound and of which the regime often appears as prisoner. They provide a set of attitudes which the government is likely to fall back on in periods of domestic or foreign policy crisis. They constitute not so much an alternative to pragmatism as a component of the difficult context in which the more pragmatic of Iran's leaders must try to conduct foreign policy. For example, President Khatami's policy of "tension reduction" with the United States, Arab neighbors, and the rest of the international community has been hardly criticized by the right-wing press and conservative clerics and members of parliament. The supreme leader himself has criticized it, directly and by implication. The head of the judiciary, who is Khamenei's appointee, and other senior clerics close to the supreme leader, have worked to undermine the new president.

The foreign policy contradictions this generates, and the dilemma the more pragmatic of Iran's policymakers face, is well illustrated by remarks of President Rafsanjani to the opening session of the new parliament in June 1996. In his speech, Rafsanjani sketched out a vista of almost unlimited economic potential for Iran, given its resources and its geographic location. In an unmistakable reference to the oil and gas projects in Azerbaijan and (until very recently) Turkmenistan from which the United States has managed to exclude the Islamic Republic, he said Iran could become the "crossroads of the world for . . . energy pipelines from East and West," if only "we showed a little prudence (*tadbir*)."[23]

This echoed remarks Rafsanjani made on his return from his tour of Sudan and Senegal and the meeting of the Organization of the Islamic Conference (OIC) in 1991. As already noted, Rafsanjani sought to depict his African tour as a triumph. Somewhat fancifully, he also sought to represent the resolutions of the OIC on the issue of the Arab-Israeli peace talks as a victory for the Iranian position—although this was far from being the case. His purpose in all this, it soon became clear, was to try to argue that Iran could achieve all its foreign policy goals, and promote the triumph of the Islamic cause, without extremism.

> The Islamic Republic now needs a prudent policy more than it needs anything else . . . so that we can have a presence and help people without being accused of engaging in terrorism, without anyone being able to call us fanatics. We have no need to speak fanatically. We have no need to chant impractical slogans . . . needlessly frightening people. We need prudently and wisely to explain Islam, the Koran, the traditions of the Prophet to the people of the world . . . We can be the leading light of the world of Islam, as long as we act with prudence and wisdom.[24]

This plea for a prudent, practical foreign policy—and for a prudent rhetoric to go with it—may be the voice of Iranian pragmatism speaking. But its claims remain large; Rafsanjani imagines Iran as "the leading light of the world of Islam" even while he is arguing that the ultimate triumph of the Islamic cause can be achieved more effectively through patient example than through extremism. Moreover, as I hope this analysis demonstrates, if the pragmatic instinct has proponents among the ruling clergy, as indicated by Khatami's policies, and if it helps shape foreign policy, it must ceaselessly compete for primacy with the powerful ideological legacy of the revolution.

ENDNOTES

1 Cited in Shaul Bakhash, "The Islamic Republic of Iran 1979-1989," *Wilson Quarterly* (Autumn 1989), 54.

2 Ibid., 58.

3 Remarks by Mohammad Reza Golpaygani, *Foreign Broadcasting Information Service, Near East and South Asia* (hereafter *FBIS/NESA*), 3 October 1991, 39, citing *Jomhuri-ye Islami*, 19 September 1991, 4.

4 See report on the letter to Gorbachev in *FBIS\NESA*, January 1989, 47-48, and a comment on its significance by Hashemi-Rafsanjani in ibid., 17 January 1989, 61-62.

5 In 1987, inept handling of the demonstrators in Mecca by the Saudi security forces led to riots. Police fired on the crowds and over 400 pilgrims died, 270 of them Iranians. Iran and Saudi Arabia broke diplomatic relations. No Iranians made the pilgrimage in 1988 and 1989; and new ground rules for Iranian pilgrims had to be agreed by the two countries before Iranian pilgrimages could be resumed.

6 A translation of Khomeini's testament appeared in three installments in *FBIS/NESA*, 6 June 1989, 41-47; 7 June 1989, 57-65; and 8 June 1989, 58-64. The quotations in this paragraph are from the issue of June 6, 44-45.

7 On the problems of succession to the post of supreme leader and challenges to Khamenei's authority, see Shaul Bakhash, "Iran: The Crisis of Legitimacy", in Martin Kramer, ed., *Middle Eastern Lectures* I (Tel-Aviv: University of Tel-Aviv Press, and Syracuse: University of Syracuse Press, 1995), 99-118.

8 *FBIS\NESA*, 17 September 1993, 49-50.

9 Remarks by Ali Akbar Nategh-Nuri, Associated Press, 1 April 1996, citing Iranian newspapers.

10 These ideas runs through much of the testament. But see especially *FBIS/NESA*, 7 June 1989, 57-58.

11 See, for example, Khamenei's message to the hajj pilgrims, which appears in translation in *FBIS/NESA*, 19, 20, and 21 June 1991.

12 Remarks by Khamenei, *FBIS/NESA*, 18 October 1991, 39.

13 Remarks by Khamenei, *FBIS/NESA*, 7 June 1995, 23 and 25.

14 Ibid., 25.

15 *FBIS/NESA,* 23 December 1991, 44.

16 *FBIS/NESA,* 23 December 1991, 46.

17 *FBIS/NESA,* 16 December 1991, 84

18 *FBIS/NESA,* 6 December 1991, 43-44.

19 *FBIS/NESA,* 5 November 1991, 82-83.

20 See, for example, Shaul Bakhash, "Iranian Politics Since the Gulf War," in Robert B. Satloff, ed., *The Politics of Change in the Middle East* (Boulder, Colo.: Westview, 1993), 63-84.

21 For Khamenei and Khatami quotations, see John Lancaster, "Iran's Top Leaders Differ on Relations With West," *Washington Post,* 10 December 1997.

22 Khatami's commitment to strengthening the rule of law and civil society at home and to "dialogue between civilizations" abroad is hardly in doubt. His most recent collection of essays, *Az Donya-ye Shahr be Shahr-e Donya [From the World of the City to the City of the World]* (Teheran. 1994) makes clear his admiration for Western political thinkers like John Locke and his arguments in favor of tolerance, liberty, individual rights, and security of life and property. But Khatami, too, has been capable of seeing the encounter between Islam and the West in harsher terms. See the essays in an earlier collection, *Bim-e Mowj [Fear of the Wave]* (Teheran: 1993).

23 *Ettelaat,* International Edition, 3 June 1996, 3.

24 *FBIS/NESA,* 23 December 1991, 46.

MEMORANDUM FOR THE PRESIDENT

From: Judith Miller

**Subject: Critical Strategic Choices in U.S. Policy
             toward Iran**

The election of Mohammad Khatami gives the United States another opportunity, indeed, an obligation to rethink its policy toward Tehran. But some modesty is in order. First, the tortured diplomatic history between Tehran and Washington shows that each side has often spectacularly misjudged the other's intentions, motivation, and capabilities. America's previous hunts for elusive "moderates" in Iran's leadership, for instance, have only wound up embarrassing Washington and undermining American credibility among regional allies.

Second, neither America nor Europe, long at odds over how to handle Iran, has proven adept at coaxing good behavior out of the mullahs. "Dual containment" may be flawed, but Europe's critical dialogue has been even less effective, and perhaps even more cynical. (In the aftermath of the Mykonos verdict, even the Europeans were humiliated into temporarily retreating from their policy.)

Third, whatever the U.S. policy's flaws, a clumsy or poorly timed shift to even a more nuanced policy may be counterproductive if it prompts Tehran to misread Washington's intentions and falsely conclude that America is now willing to tolerate Iranian mischief in exchange for commercial advantage—which is, after all, the message of Europe's allegedly constructive engagement—or is tired of playing regional policeman (or Richard Haass's "reluctant sheriff") and has lost its determination to protect its strategic interests in the region.

Good policy should be grounded in an appreciation of the revolution's development—as outlined in my first memo—and an acknowledgment that America's ability to affect Iran's current behavior, let alone its future political evolution, may be marginal at best. What do we know about the Iranian regime so far? To sum up my previous arguments:

1. The revolution in its most dangerous expansionist phase has been over for years. Whether one dates its waning to the Ayatollah's decla-

ration of the supremacy of Iran's interests over those of Islam—or "Islam is what we say it is"—or Ayatollah Khomeini's death, or the constitutional amendments, or even to Ed Shirley's soccer riots, the Iran of today is different from and in many respects weaker than it was when the Ayatollah Khomeini came to power. While the "revolution," as a means of freeing Iran from foreign dominance, is still respected, the Islamic government is not. The revolution is corrupt and has failed to provide prosperity or freedom. The level of disenchantment is so great as to threaten Iran's commitment not only to clerical rule but also to Islam. If a real vote were ever held on whether Qum should rule, the mullahs would probably lose as decisively as Khatami won.

At the same time, Iran has continued (indeed intensified) some of the activities of greatest concern to Washington and the West—among them, its pursuit of weapons of mass destruction. Iran has also increased direct support for international terrorism and its efforts to sabotage the Arab-Israeli peace process. Why has it done this? Perhaps in response to Iran's perpetual fear of encirclement—an Iranian version of the best defense is a good offense. In the case of nuclear weapons, one could argue that Iran is simply reverting to its traditional national-ist agenda. Tehran's nuclear program, after all, was started by the Shah. It could be the result of its failures in most other spheres. Sometimes all that seemingly remains of the revolution is its determination not to be defeated, or even seduced by the Great and Little Satans. But given how poorly we understand Iranian motivations, it's hard to rule any explanation out, particularly in the absence of any direct contact. But Iran, though exhausted, is still dangerous.

2. Iran, and young Iran, in particular, is obsessed with America. Perhaps calling the obsession a love-hate relationship, apart from being a cliché, is too strong, but America in the mind of Iran looms large. Everything we wear, say, and do is watched and debated in Tehran. The obsession, moreover, is long-standing. Properly used, it could be a source of leverage in Tehran.

3. Khatami is the result of a protest vote. The reason that neither Washington nor Tehran anticipated his triumph is that policymakers in both capitals failed to appreciate the level of disdain for the ruling clergy and the desire for a change.

4. Khatami is a cleric, an organization man. Like Gorbachev—and the analogy has been much overused—he wants to reform the system, not junk it. But his writings and statements suggest that he fears Iran has only a limited time left to develop what he calls a "new" Islamic civilization before its Islamic adventure collapses. He argues that the great Islamic civilization of yore is dead—that it cannot be resurrected, an unusual thought in fundamentalist circles. He wants to make his Islamic government more modern, efficient, and politically flexible, and less corrupt and socially oppressive.

Some say all he is likely to achieve is a more relaxed social atmosphere and fewer Islamic restrictions—a safety valve. They worry that the West would be no better off, in fact, perhaps even worse off, if Khatami succeeds in reducing public antipathy toward the clergy while freeing the government to continue its misbehavior abroad. But Khatami seems more ambitious than that. And in any event, while many Iranians, especially the young, voted for him so that women could wear lipstick and men could drink home-brewed alcohol with friends in their homes without fear, many of his supporters voted against the stagnation of the current system and for a better economy. To do anything about that, Khatami will have to reform Iran's centrally controlled and highly subsidized economic system. University slots and jobs will have to be awarded on merit, rather than as a reward for "Islamically correct" behavior, for instance.

Iranian statistics may be as credible as Tehran's denials of sponsoring terrorism, but economically, the country is doing no more than muddling through. Tehran has been unable to woo back the two to four million entrepreneurs and technocrats who have fled, for instance, and according to the World Bank, corruption has become so endemic as to threaten domestic and foreign investment. Eliyahu Kanovsky, an Israeli professor, estimates that Iran's subsidies now total some $15 billion, roughly equal to the country's 1995 oil revenues, and the IMF adds that while subsidies may keep life for the poor bearable, domestic energy subsidies alone account for roughly 7 to 8 percent of GDP. In sum, Khatami will have his work cut out for him.

We don't really know what he will try to do in foreign affairs. He has written that he does not believe in confronting the West through violence and terror. And among his cabinet appointees was Ataollah Mohajerani, minister of Islamic guidance and culture, known for his desire for better ties to the West. But we also do not know whether Khatami, even if he wants to, will be able to overturn the consensus on Iran's foreign policy course that has prevailed under the "first" and "second" republics. He faces competing power centers, of which he is just one, albeit one backed for now by demonstrable popular support.

So a key question to be asked is: Does the U.S. policy of dual containment reflect these new realities and the complexity of Iran's predicament today? I think not.

First, dual containment may not mean that the United States equates Iran and Iraq, but any policy that gives Iranian hard-liners an opportunity to argue that it does is, at very least, poorly named, badly presented, and easily misinterpreted. In other words, it's bad PR. And these things do matter in Iran. Even Patrick Clawson, a staunch proponent of sanctions, argued recently on Capitol Hill that the United States is "losing the propaganda war" against Tehran, that most people in the Middle East, Europe, and even the United States hold Washington responsible for refusing to talk to Iran. As a result, he argues, Iran has no reason to believe that its foreign policy cannot be sustained. Washington should make it clear that in its view, these two regimes are not equivalent. Would 70 percent of Iraqis ever be permitted to elect a moderate vice president critical of Saddam Hussein? How many Arab countries have real elections at all?

Second, even as the Iranian revolution has lost political steam and much of its support at home and abroad, Washington's policy towards Tehran, though marked by fits and starts, has become steadily harsher over time.

One might be able to defend tighter restrictions if the administration had decided that they were an appropriate response to Iranian misconduct. Martin Kramer, for instance, has argued that the tougher U.S. stance is a natural response to America's changing and ever broadening role in the region since the collapse of the Soviet Union. With the Russian threat gone—at least temporarily—Washington could turn its attention to doing more than keeping the Soviets out: it could pursue its traditional twin objectives—keeping oil flowing freely at acceptable prices (known euphemistically as stabilizing the region) and protecting Israel—by promoting an ambitious peace between Israel and the Arabs and greater economic openness in the region. Hence, he argues, Iran's fierce opposition to this strategic goal, the U.S. "master plan," he calls it (or dare we say America's "new world order") has made Iran a far greater challenge than it was before the end of the Cold War, and deserving of stricter American containment efforts.

As both America and Iran would like to remake the region in their own image, a confrontation may be unavoidable. But the argument would be more persuasive if Iran were not so much weaker than the United States, and if current policy, in fact, reflected Martin Kramer's cool, dispassionate analysis. Alas, it does not. The administration has imposed greater restrictions on Iran mainly because it chose not to challenge a Congress that found it politically expedient in the aftermath of the TWA 800 crash to find a plausible scapegoat. The FBI may now have concluded that the crash was not to terrorism at all, but the sanctions remain.

I'm not opposed to the sanctions against Iran, per se. But for a moment, consider America's policy as Iranians see it, based on my conversations with Iranians who say they favor closer ties to the United States. What was Washington's response to Iran's relatively good behavior during the Gulf war and its immediate aftermath? To Rafsanjani's help with hostages in Lebanon? How did the United States react to the Iranian government's decision to award a one billion dollar contract to repair and expand its oil fields to Conoco only a few weeks after the deal was announced? By signing the Iran-Libya Sanctions Act (ILSA) of 1996. Assuming that President Rafsanjani was trying to signal Iran's interest in an "authoritative" dialogue that the United States claims it wants, ILSA would surely undermine his argument that concessions or signals of this kind would be positively received in Washington. The administration says it wants a dialogue with Iran, but given Tehran's paranoid sensitivity to perceived slights and its anxiety about maintaining its dignity and independence, why should the mullahs condone dialogue with a country whose laws are aimed at isolating and, if lucky, destroying it? In the words of Richard Murphy, the former assistant secretary of state who helped prepare the administration's Irangate policy in the late 1980s, America's invitation to dialogue, in light of its own harsh rhetoric and action, is "unpersuasive."

Robert Satloff has argued that Iran, in fact, does not seek a dialogue with Washington, that such contacts would undermine whatever shred of ideological credibility the hard-liners have left. That may be true. But if so, why not put the onus of rejecting a dialogue squarely on Iran? Why not increase the divisions within the ruling elite by forcing a debate on a public American proposal for a dialogue not only about terrorism and the behavior to which America objects, but economic ties, repatriated assets, and at least some of the items on Iran's agenda?

I doubt that hard-liners would permit such a dialogue at the moment, but who knows? What does the United States lose by suggesting one?

Proposing to send a deputy secretary to Geneva or Oman for such a meeting, as Anthony Cordesman has noted, would not require the United States to abandon its efforts to contain Tehran militarily. It would not even require the United States to abandon sanctions. At the very least, it would be a way of improving America's credibility in the ongoing propaganda war. It might also drive a wider wedge between young Iranians and their government. In other words, we could do what our Gulf allies say Iran does so well, as Murphy put it, "smile and subvert."

I see little downside in making a serious offer to discuss our differences with the largest nation in the Persian Gulf the next time Khatami does something impressive, and a great deal possibly to be gained.

What other choices does the U.S. have?

1. Continue the current policy.

Some analysts argue that the policy is working fine—that dual containment's sanctions were responsible for Khatami's election. I can only conclude that most people who say this have never set foot in Iran. It is both wrong and arrogant. Most economists who have looked closely at this question conclude that at most sanctions have only imposed additional costs on the Iranian economy. Fine. It has also managed to delay some contracts for the development of Iranian oil and gas, though this appears to be as much the result of tough Iranian bargaining as sanctions. But as economist Jeffrey Schott and Sarah Miller, of *Petroleum Intelligence Weekly*, told Congress in July, these delays have not reduced oil income and will not lower Iranian oil production. Iranian oil production actually increased in 1996-1997 from levels a few years earlier.

Patrick Clawson argues that the sanctions are aimed at the Achilles' heel of the Iranian regime: oil production. But does the United States really want to use sanctions that diminish the supply of a vital resource whose price we wish to stabilize and reduce? Washington should want more oil flowing on the market, not less. And it should want oil and gas that flows through a variety of pipelines in a number of different countries, so that neither Russia nor any other single country has a stranglehold on this strategic resource. This was yet another advantage of Washington's recent decision not to oppose the construction of the new gas pipeline from Turkmenistan through Iran to Turkey.

Sanctions have a cost for America as well. Schott estimates that the current U.S. exports to the 26 countries subject to U.S. sanctions in 1995 were $15 to $19 billion lower than they would have been in the absence of sanctions.

Finally, there is a consensus that the sanctions, at least so far, seem to have induced no significant change in the Iranian behavior Washington wishes to change.

I suppose sanctions are an appropriate response when one doesn't know what else to do. But it is unlikely they will have a severe effect as long as Europe will not join America in this policy.

2. Military action.

This option is one that is obviously being considered in light of possible Iranian complicity in the Khobar Towers bombing in Dhahran.

Most analysts argue, however, that the United States is unlikely to find proof of Iranian involvement—which is widely presumed. This may be fortunate. Even Uri Lubrani of Israel, who has been in charge of the war against Hezbollah in Lebanon for years, recently warned a group of Washington policymakers that nothing would rally Iranians more around their hard-line line government than a military strike.

America's Gulf allies have also warned Washington that they would be the likely targets of retribution by an infuriated Iran—and, therefore, are not enthusiastic about military action either.

3. Refine or modify sanctions.

The United States could add creative disincentives to its policy. Uri Lubrani has suggested one: trying to pressure Iran through Syria, which has long sought concessions from the United States. Damascus, after all, calls the shots in Lebanon and could contain Hezbollah if it wanted to, which would strain Syrian relations with Tehran. At the moment it is not willing to do that, but a breakthrough in the peace process that would re-engage Syria would revive this now dormant option.

Another possibility is increased and nastier covert action if Iran continues its support for terrorism and other mischief. Ed Shirley, for instance, notes that the CIA never really tried to reinforce Persian awe of American power by, say, fomenting separatist passions in Iran's far-flung outposts, such as resource-rich Azerbaijan. Iran, like Iraq, fears territorial dismemberment. Such action, at very least, might unhinge the clerics and warn them that America is prepared to make Tehran's life miserable if terrorism, etcetera, does not stop.

Some analysts have suggested pressuring Tehran through the Taliban in Afghanistan, with whom Tehran has been at odds. But this smacks somewhat of Washington's earlier effort to play off Iraq against Iran, which ended badly. And the Taliban, too, pose their own potential regional challenge to the United States.

Sanctions could be more closely targeted against Tehran's pursuit of nuclear and biochemical technology. Washington has already made some modest progress convincing its European allies that such controls are very much in their interest. This effort could be intensified.

On balance, options for affecting Iran's behavior are rather limited. We can keep sanctions on, or refine them, knowing that this will be effective mainly at the margins. We can maintain our policy but change our tone, and openly seek dialogue and see what happens. And America can and must continue to try to rescue its beleaguered Arab-Israeli peace process. The late Yitzhak Rabin firmly believed that the best way to confront Iran was through its isolation as the result of the prosperity and stability that would come from peace between the Arabs and Israel. The current crisis gives Iran opportunities for mischief that would not exist if Arabs and Israelis were not questioning their counterpart's commitment to the Oslo peace process. It is essential to American interests in the region that the peace process be revived.

Iran itself, I believe, must and eventually will conclude that it is tired of being an international outlaw: Iran, an old and great civilization, hates being ignored, kept on the periphery of world events. One day, it will want to be included among conventionally civilized states. It will want to become a normal country.

MEMORANDUM FOR THE PRESIDENT

From: **Shaul Bakhash**

Subject: **Critical Strategic Choices in U.S. Policy
             toward Iran**

This report recommends that the U.S. government actively explore the possibilities of a dialogue with Iran; that it do so in the framework of formal negotiations; and that it be prepared to offer Iran economic and diplomatic concessions/incentives in return for Iranian steps to deal with issues of greatest concern to the United States.

There is a rationale for a change in the U.S. posture toward Iran. Sanctions have hurt Iran but not sufficiently to cause it to alter policy in those areas of greatest import to the United States; there are fractures within the Iranian leadership that the United States should exploit; Iran might be weaned away from those policies that seem most inimical to U.S. interests by a policy of carrot and as well as stick; and the moment is opportune for a change in the U.S. position due to the internal political dynamics brought about by the election of a new president.

1. The effect of sanctions has been limited.

Critics of the containment/sanctions policy against Iran argue that it should be abandoned because it is ineffective. This allegation is inaccurate. Sanctions have hurt Iran. But they have not hurt Iran sufficiently to cause it to alter policy in those areas of greatest concern to the United States.

On the plus side, from the U.S. perspective, the containment/sanctions policy has considerably curtailed Iran's weapons acquisition and its economic programs. Iran cannot buy weapons in Western Europe. In part due to American prodding, Germany agreed not to complete the construction of nuclear reactors at Bushire—a project originally launched under the monarchy. Japan postponed payment of the second $500-million installment of a loan for a hydroelectric power plant. World Bank loans to Iran would have been considerably higher but for American opposition. American monitoring has slowed the transfer of nuclear and dual-use technology to Iran. The Islamic Republic was successfully excluded from the consortium that will develop Azerbaijan's oil. U.S. sanctions have increased the costs for Iran of obtaining certain types of equipment and technology and reinforce a climate unfavorable to foreign investment.

More importantly, the Iran-Libya Sanctions Act (ILSA) has helped discourage investment in Iran's oil and gas industry. Foreign investment is crucial if Iran is to expand current levels of oil and gas production and secure the foreign exchange urgently needed for large-scale investment in industry and infrastructure. Only 2 of the 11 large oil- and gas-related projects put out for international tender by Iran two years ago have been taken up by foreign investors. British Petroleum, Italy's ENI, France's Elf Aquitaine, and Japanese and other companies have avoided involvement in these projects. Royal Dutch/Shell has been discussing several large gas projects with Iran, but is not about to sign any agreements.

On the other hand, the last few years have also displayed the limits of sanctions policy. Iran was able to secure arms from China, Russia, and Korea, nuclear plants from Russia, and nuclear technology from Russia and China. The French firm Total SA took up the $600-million contract to develop the Sirri offshore oil and gas fields that Conoco was obliged to abandon in 1995 due to a presidential order banning U.S. investments in Iran. Total SA has signed a second $2-billion deal to help develop Iran's huge South Pars gas field. Malaysia's state-owned oil company, Petronas, and Russia's Gazprom took a 30 percent stake in this project—*after* passage of ILSA. While the project under which Turkey was to purchase $23 billion of Iranian gas over 20 years now appears moot (Turkey will secure its gas from Turkmenistan instead), the Iran-Turkey agreement indicates that even close U.S. allies may be willing to flaunt, or find ways around, sanctions legislation. In fact, U.S. acquiescence in the Turkmenistan-Turkey gas deal, which involves gas being piped through Iran to Turkey, was actuated in part by the desire to prevent Turkey from turning to Iran for gas supplies. In 1993-94, the European countries and Japan rescheduled the major portion of Iran's outstanding foreign debt. In 1997, French entities extended nearly $500 million of new credits to Iran, and a syndicate of German banks agreed to lend an Iranian engineering company $90 million to rebuild an offshore oil platform damaged during the war with Iraq. In the last few years, Iran has carefully and successfully cultivated ties with the countries of the European Union (EU), particularly Germany, and also with other major states (Russia, China, India) as counterweights to U.S. influence. It has begun to cultivate better relations with Saudi Arabia and other Persian Gulf states—and the Saudis, for one, are responding favorably.

It would thus be difficult to argue that the United States has succeeded in isolating Iran. The Islamic Republic recently played a role in mediating the conflict in Tajikistan. It is a player in Afghanistan's internal politics, as it has been in Lebanon's. It earned goodwill among Bosnia's Muslims by providing them with financial aid and military equipment when few others were willing to help. The Mykonos trial in Berlin in April 1997, in which Germany's federal authorities implicated Iran's highest officials in the 1992 assassination of the leader of Iran's Kurdish Democratic Party, led to a suspension of the EU's "constructive dialogue" with Iran and strained Iran's relations with EU states. But these strains are likely to be short-lived. The EU ambassadors, who were withdrawn from Tehran after the Mykonos trial judgment, are now back in the Iranian capital.

Nor have sanctions crippled Iran's financial ability to fund radical movements abroad, for the simple reason that the cost to Iran is not unduly high (say $100-150 million annually) when measured against oil revenues of $14 billion a year. True, Iran pays a heavy long-term price. It sacrifices potential international investment for foreign policy radicalism. Iran's technocrats are keenly aware of this, as is Iran's new President Khatami. But Iran's clerical leaders do not often conduct cost-benefit studies; and there is no real public debate on the issue. No Iranian politician makes the dramatic argument in public that Iran's foreign policy results in investments not made, jobs not created, a lagging oil industry, unmodernized factories, or a shortage of schools and housing.

Moreover, Iran has weathered the debt/foreign exchange crisis of 1993-94; the economy lumbers along; there is no abject poverty or starvation;

and oil revenues are adequate, at least in the near term, to mask extensive mismanagement, corruption, and waste. Those of Iran's leaders who choose to do so can overlook the economic effects of sanctions.

ILSA is deeply resented by America's European allies, who lodged a complaint with the World Trade Organization and are threatening retaliatory measures. In the long run, ILSA may not succeed in blocking new investment in Iran's energy sector anyway. According to testimony in July 1997 before the House International Relations Committee by Sarah Miller, editor in chief of *Petroleum Intelligence Weekly,* the dearth of foreign investment in Iran's oil and gas industry has been due as much to tough Iranian terms as to U.S. sanctions. Miller believes that the situation could change rapidly, and the oil companies would scramble to invest in Iran, if the Islamic Republic offered more lucrative terms—as it might well do—and allowed foreign oil firms to develop land-based as well as offshore fields.

In the wake of the embarrassment caused the Islamic Republic by the findings at the Mykonos trial, it seems unlikely that Iran will continue to assassinate its dissidents abroad. But that outcome is due more to the courage of the German judiciary than to U.S. sanctions. In fact, sanctions have not brought about an end to Iran's nuclear weapons program, its strident opposition to the Arab-Israeli peace process, or its support for radical Islamic movements.

2. The United States should exploit fractures in the Iranian leadership.

Iran pursues policies of great concern to the United States. It is seeking to develop weapons of mass destruction, although these programs appear neither as advanced nor as large as was once assumed. It is acquiring long-range missiles. It opposes the Arab-Israeli peace process both through inflammatory rhetoric and by support for groups that use violence to disrupt peace efforts. It has been linked to terrorist acts abroad. It kills Iranian dissidents on foreign soil. These policies are deeply imbedded in revolutionary ideology, Iran's sense of its worldwide Islamic mission, and the institutional culture of powerful organizations such as the Revolutionary Guards. Iran will not abandon such positions easily.

However, Iran's narrow leadership is not of one piece. It is divided on both domestic and foreign policy issues. These divisions have been much in evidence since the death of Ayatollah Khomeini in 1989. To cite a couple of examples: In the 1992 parliamentary elections, a conservative clerical faction was able to almost completely shut out the economic radicals that had until then dominated parliament and government. Last year, a group of high government officials and technocrats, associated with outgoing president Rafsanjani, broke in turn with the conservative clerics and formed their own political movement, the Servants of Construction, and contested the 1996 parliamentary elections on a platform of economic development and technocratic excellence—thus de-emphasizing ideological and revolutionary purity. In the current parliament, the dominant faction of conservative clerics vies not only with the Servants of Construction, but also with economic radicals, who favor state control of the economy and wealth distribution, and Islamicists who would aggressively export the revolution and are dead-set against any accommodation with the United States.

We have in Iran a politics of competing elites, not an open political system. Real opposition parties are not permitted to operate. Nevertheless, the factionalism of the inner group provides openings that an imaginative U.S. policy can exploit. Those in the leadership who have argued for an accommodation with the United States have had a difficult time of it. From the perspective of Tehran's hard-liners, the United States appears unalterably opposed to Iran, determined not only to "contain" it but to strangle it economically. Officials in the inner circle who argued for offering the Sirri oil exploration contract to Conoco lost credibility when President Clinton effectively banned the agreement. The proponents in the government of a dialogue with the United States would be strengthened if it appeared there was some give in the American position, if American policy were more nuanced.

Moreover, although the public discussion of certain subjects is virtually taboo (not surprisingly, these taboo subjects include the activities of the security agencies, terrorism, arms policy, and, to a lesser degree, foreign policy), Iran nevertheless has a lively daily and periodical press. Parliament can be rambunctious. There are quasi-organized and organized groups and professional associations (Muslim student associations, trade union organizations, etc.) that speak out on public issues and maneuver among the major political factions represented in parliament.

These divisions were much in evidence during the spring election campaign for president and since the balloting in May.

3. The election of a new president is a hopeful sign.

Mohammad Khatami was elected as Iran's new president in May 1997, in a stunning upset victory that caught both Iranians and foreign observers by surprise. Some 80 percent of the electorate went to the polls, a figure almost without precedent since the early years of the revolution. Khatami received nearly 70 percent of the ballot, securing 20 million votes to only 7 million for the favored front-runner, Ali Akbar Nategh-Nouri. Ayatollah Nategh-Nouri, the speaker of the *majlis,* or parliament, had been endorsed by most of the leading clerics, several high officials, and implicitly, by the leader, Ayatollah Khamenei, himself.

The vote for Khatami has rightly been interpreted as a vote against the ruling establishment; for change; for relief from the social, cultural, and political restrictions the regime has imposed on society, and for improved economic conditions. Khatami galvanized the public with a campaign that emphasized respect for the rule of law and individual rights, tolerance for a multiplicity of views, and the strengthening of civil society. Khatami rejected the idea of a "clash of civilizations," stressed the need for "dialogue between civilizations," and said Iranians have much to learn from the West.

A former minister of Islamic guidance who was ousted in 1992 because his policies toward film, theater, the arts, and book and magazine publishing were considered too liberal, Khatami is of course still a member of the ruling elite. He does not intend to undo the present system, but to reform it. He has repeatedly emphasized the centrality of Islam to the very character of the Islamic Republic. When he stresses respect for the constitution, he implies both the rule of law and a framework which provides for clerical supremacy. Nevertheless, he is attempting to strike a balance between constitutional requirements that vest ultimate authority in the hands of the *faqih,* or Islamic jurist, and individual rights, between the requirements of Islam and the idea of civil society. He is firm on the need for the rule of law, protection of individual rights, and strengthening civic associations. His election has introduced a degree of fluidity in Iranian politics.

Khatami has drawn around himself a group of advisers who have other priorities than opposing the Arab-Israeli peace process or fulminating against the United States, who desire more normal traffic with the West and Washington, and who are keenly aware of the need for Iran to attract foreign investment.

Since taking office, Khatami has pursued a foreign policy, in his words, of "tension reduction" and "dialogue between civilizations." He has assiduously courted the Arab states of the Persian Gulf. He has worked hard to repair relations with the European community. Most dramatically, in a CNN interview in January 1998, he called for a "constructive dialogue" and "cultural exchanges" with the United States, and for steps, on both sides, to break "the wall of suspicion" between the two countries. Since then, Iranian officials have given other indications of a desire to work toward an improvement of relations with Washington. For example, an American team was invited to participate in a wrestling competition in Tehran in February. That same month, American academics and members of the nongovernmental policy community took part in a policy conference in the Iranian capital. Both groups were warmly received.

There is, of course, no guarantee that Khatami will prevail over regime hard-liners. However, if Khatami manages to ease control over the press, theater, cinema, and cultural affairs, strengthen civic associations, permit greater participation by nonclerical groups in politics, and rein in the vigilante groups (admittedly, a very tall order), he will strengthen the moderate forces in society. He has already created an environment in which foreign policy can be more openly debated, and there is strong evidence that Khatami's America initiative is hugely popular. Even groups considered "radical," such as Islamic student associations, have endorsed Khatami's policy of an "inter-civilizational dialogue," and Khatami has strong support for seeking a dialogue with the United States among a portion of Tehran's influential press.

4. Khatami, however, faces formidable obstacles.

As president, Khatami is not Iran's ultimate authority, a role reserved for the leader, Ayatollah Khamenei. In recent years, Khamenei has taken the lead in denouncing the United States and the Arab-Israeli peace process, in depicting Israel as an illegitimate state, and in attacking what in Iran is described as the "Western cultural onslaught." Khamenei has consolidated his hand over foreign policy, the military, and the security agencies. Khatami will not be able to make major changes in foreign or security policy without Khamenei's acquiescence. Khamenei appears to have acquiesced in Khatami's America initiative, but only grudgingly. He has made several speeches ruling out a dialogue, let alone diplomatic relations, with the United States. The new president faces a parliamentary majority that is conservative on social issues, friendly to the bazaar merchants but suspicious of entrepreneurial capital, and not comfortable with the idea of open traffic with the West. This strong opposition explains why, in his CNN interview, Khatami for the moment ruled out government-to-government negotiations and diplomatic relations with the United States, opting instead for cultural exchanges as a means of breaking the "wall of suspicion" between the two countries.

The security agencies, led by the ministry of intelligence, have considerable power. They are responsible for the repression of the intelligentsia at home, the killing of dissidents abroad, and support for groups abroad that engage in violence or terrorist acts. It seems very unlikely that Khatami will achieve control over the security agencies, but he may be able to persuade Khamenei to rein them in. Khatami has appointed as minister of interior a person with whom he is comfortable.

In addition, vested interests are firmly entrenched. The Foundation for the Disinherited and other para-statal foundations control hundreds of industries and business enterprises and stand in the way of privatization and economic rationalization. Senior clerics and their relatives are direct or sleeping partners in business enterprises. The security agencies are developing commercial and business interests as well. The Revolutionary Guards command identifies with the clerical establishment. The bureaucracy is huge, inefficient, and corrupt.

Already the long knives are out for Khatami. The conservative press has attacked his idea of dialogue and cultural exchanges with the United States. The supreme leader himself, as noted, has described dialogue with the United States as contrary to the interests of Iran, Islam, and the revolution. Clerics close to Khamenei have sought, in ways direct and indirect, to undermine Khatami's authority.

5. Khatami also has considerable strengths.

Khatami received a resounding popular mandate. People across a wide spectrum of classes seem to respond to him. Public expectations in the wake of his election are enormously high. This could prove damaging to Khatami if he fails to deliver on his promise of change. But public discontent might as easily be directed at the regime itself, if it appeared that Khatami's plans were being frustrated by the uncooperative attitude of Khamenei, parliament, and other political factions. This provides the leader and parliament with some incentive to cooperate with the new president.

In the *majlis*, Khatami will also have the support of a faction of some 100-odd deputies in the 270-seat house. Khatami's supporters are not in the majority. But they are articulate and energetic; and power and patronage may attract more adherents to the president's side. Khatami can count on the support of the outgoing president, Rafsanjani. Khatami has been a Rafsanjani protégé, and Rafsanjani is bound to favor many of Khatami's policies.

Rafsanjani, it is true, is not always a reliable ally; and his own efforts at "pragmatism" during his eight-year presidency met with middling success. His privatization program suffered something akin to partial-birth abortion. During his tenure, the anti-American, anti-Israeli rhetoric and the assassination of Iranians abroad intensified. He was not able to put the Rushdie issue to rest. He did nothing in the last three years to stop the suddenly heightened mistreatment of writers and intellectuals by the security agencies.

On the other hand, Iran today is a different country than eight years ago. Some privatization has taken place. Women are more visible in society and the workplace, their legal rights have been strengthened, and they are less often harassed on the streets (or they continue to be harassed but are not hauled off and subjected to lashings for infractions of the dress code as in the past). The press is freer. It was on Rafsanjani's watch that Iran resumed diplomatic relations with the "hateful" monarchies of Saudi Arabia, Jordan, and Morocco and with the Egypt of the nefarious Camp David accords. During the Gulf war, Rafsanjani adopted a position very close to that of the U.S.-led alliance—in the face of demands by some radical members of parliament that Iran form an alliance with Iraq against the United States.

Rafsanjani is implicated in the full range of Iran's foreign policies over the last eight years and longer. But he has his pragmatic side. Rafsanjani also remains politically adept and influential. He will head the awkwardly named Council for Determining the Interests of the Islamic Republic, which has been charged with setting broad policies for the country. If Rafsanjani is not always steadfast, his support will nevertheless be important to Khatami.

6. A period of turmoil?

Khatami is facing strong opposition and obstruction in his attempt to redirect domestic and foreign policy. Iran is entering a period of muted internal factionalism: conflict over the control of key organizations and policies. The direction in which the leader, Khamenei, and other influential clerics and leading political figures tilt in these disputes will matter; so, to a degree that is at the moment unclear, will public opinion. In the first year of the revolution, in 1979, Khomeini gave currency to the phrase, "the army of 20 million," to refer to the entire younger generation who were supposedly ready to rise to the defense of the revolution and the Islamic Republic. Today, some of the press has taken up the same phrase to refer to the "army of 20 million" who voted for Khatami, and some of Khatami's supporters suggest they will take to the streets if he is blocked at every turn. This public mood may pass, but the possibility that rival factions will appeal to the streets cannot be ruled out.

7. Administration policy has so far been right on the mark.

The U.S. administration has responded cautiously but positively to Khatami's election. Both the president and the secretary of state have described the elections as a positive sign. President Clinton, in his message to Muslims at the end of the fasting period of Ramadan in February 1997, said he was never happy with the estrangement between the American and the Iranian people, described the problems between the two countries as "not insurmountable," and looked to the reestablishment of relations between the two countries in the future. At the same time, the United States has continued to oppose Iran's attempts to acquire missile and nuclear technology and to express concern over Iran's support for groups involved in terrorism and Iran's opposition to the Arab-Israeli peace process. This position strikes the right note. It reserves the administration's position on issues of moment to the United States, but it signals a desire to encourage a process of dialogue and rapprochement.

8. A framework for dialogue/negotiations is essential.

However, something more than vague public statements, whose message can be ambiguous, is needed. Gestures made in a vacuum may lead nowhere. At his inauguration in 1989, President Bush used the phrase "good will breeds good will" in the attempt to enlist Iranian assistance for the release of American hostages in Lebanon. Rafsanjani helped secure the release of these hostages, but, at least from the Iranian perspective, there was no reciprocal American goodwill gesture. On the contrary, the American attitude toward Iran seemed to harden. Rafsanjani's policy of (timid) rapprochement suffered as a result. Iran claims it meant its offer to Conoco as a signal to the American government; but it never made this clear to Washington. As a result, any signal Tehran intended to send was lost on Washington.

If the United States intends to test the possibility of a dialogue with Iran and its new president, then such a message needs to be conveyed clearly through intermediaries (Switzerland? Germany? Saudi Arabia?). Some thought needs to be given to a framework for negotiations and to initial confidence-building steps—a further lessening of rhetoric, concessions on minor issues, for example—to be followed by discussions on issues of substance. Dual containment and sanctions were adopted to persuade Iran to change its behavior in a number of areas. Negotiations would test whether an offer of the gradual easing of sanctions and containment in exchange for reciprocal Iranian measures would achieve the same end.

MEMORANDUM FOR THE PRESIDENT

From: Your Staff

Subject: Summary of Discussion on America and Iran

This is our summary. It may not necessarily reflect everyone's views, and some may disagree with the conclusions.

1. Iran's Islamic revolution has run its course; its original aspirations have not been attained. This perspective is widely shared, both in Iran and by Muslims outside Iran, and is the judgment on both its policies at home and its efforts to spread Islamic revolutions abroad. Differences among Persians and Arabs, both Muslims, remain strong. Iran's 1997 presidential elections, although limited in scope, reflected the high level of public frustration. The political base of the regime is narrow.

2. Still, the Iranian government could become more reckless if it either perceives itself as more marginal or seeks adventures that will redeem Islamic credentials being placed in question by reforms at home. The ideological strain in Iranian foreign policy will remain important, but the United States should expect a constant dialectic between Islamic ideology and pragmatism.

3. The most worrisome threats posed to America by Iran appear to be international terrorism directed against Iran's enemies (and against Americans) and Iran's development of weapons of mass destruction. Opinion was divided about whether Iran was or was not a critical variable in the success of the Arab-Israeli peace process. Some participants also noted that Iranian oil production, and Iranian support for Caspian Basin development, was critical to American and Western energy needs.

4. Most participants did not believe that current U.S. policy, centered on diplomatic and economic isolation of Iraq using unilateral economic sanctions, was either effective in changing Iranian behavior or sustainable over the long term. The sharpest criticisms focused on the quixotic unilateralism of the policy and pointed to the disparate

policies not only of European states but also by Russia, Japan, and—a player of growing importance—China.

5. Any discussion of policy alternatives is shadowed, at the moment, by the ongoing investigation of the Al Khobar bombing, and a possible finding of Iranian culpability. Should such culpability be found, some participants thought a very strong, forceful retaliation would be warranted against Iran, and that such firmness would, over time, improve the prospects for meaningful dialogue between America and Iran. Other participants doubted the Clinton administration's ability to carry out action with adequate resolve, believed that it would be difficult to find suitable targets or obtain needed allied support, and were otherwise skeptical about punitive action. Analogies were invoked to the Beirut bombings of 1983, the 1986 raid on Libya, and the 1988 bombing of the Pan Am flight over Lockerbie. Yet participants agreed on two points: (1) the American public would insist on some response; and (2) the worst possible choice would be an ineffectual, symbolic "pinprick" of violent action (implicit references to the U.S. strikes against Iraq launched in January 1993 and September 1996, or the U.S. strikes against Syria during the Lebanon crisis).

6. Looking beyond Al Khobar, many thought the United States should publicly offer, and be seen to offer in a plain, visible way, a dialogue with Iran without preconditions. The terms for such a dialogue would include a discussion of Iran's worrying international behavior and steps to build confidence between the two nations. The United States should be willing to consider narrowing the scope of sanctions to parameters that could command multilateral support, focused on weapons development but permitting investment in and expansion of oil production. This dialogue, as in the decades of diplomacy with the Soviet Union, would be balanced by a continued posture of political and military readiness to deter and respond to unacceptable Iranian actions. In other words, the United States should tone down its rhetoric against Iran and let forces within work for change. One Arab participant recalled Theodore Roosevelt's dictum: "Speak softly, but carry a big stick."

7. If a meaningful dialogue is rejected by Iran, the United States should still seek to work with its allies to test whether "engagement"

produces positive results. Washington might start by: (1) agreeing to disagree on engagement, but (2) developing criteria with our allies to test whether their engagement works; and (3) sticking together on sanctions related to development of weapons of mass destruction. Under any circumstances, the United States should also reinvigorate discussions of energy policy with its allies.

8. Expectations for the results of such an alternative policy were low. The attitude toward the new Khatami presidency was hopeful, very attentive, but wary. Participants thought leading officials in both Iran and America would be preoccupied by domestic issues or the domestic implications of their international moves. They further questioned the real degree of control any single Iranian leader might have over the various agencies of the government and the clergy, especially the security ministries. The limited control would complicate any capacity to deliver on diplomatic bargains. Nevertheless, the alternative policy offered greater prospects than the current approach and would be more sustainable among America's allies in Europe, Asia, and the Middle East.

9. To make an alternative policy effective and sustainable, the administration will need to persuade a core group in Congress and work with that group to increase the administration's freedom to adjust sanctions in a graduated and timely fashion.

Question: What have the U.S. economic sanctions against Iran accomplished? What Iranian actions would justify ending the sanctions?

AMERICA AND TURKEY

MEMORANDUM FOR THE PRESIDENT

From: Your Staff

Subject: Questions for Discussion on America and Turkey

1. Should American leaders give much more of their attention to Turkey?

   • Can Turkey contribute significantly to achievement of U.S. policy objectives in Central Asia and the Middle East?

   • Would Turkish instability or a dramatic change in Turkey's political orientation threaten vital interests of the United States?

2. Should the United States change its policies on specific issues of importance to Turkey?

   • Should the United States sell Turkey the arms it wishes to buy?

   • Should the United States push Turkey to accept an American-mediated solution to the conflict in Cyprus?

   • Should the United States attempt to reconstruct a policy for aiding Kurdish struggles for autonomy either in Turkey or Iraq?

   • Should the United States consider a new policy to aid Turkish economic development?

3. How should the United States respond to Turkey's domestic political problems?

   A. With "aggressive engagement" to show support for and solidarity with Turkey's current government?

   B. By distancing itself from the current government, opposing a ban on Refah, urging more democratic sharing of power and greater respect for human rights and the rule of law?

   C. With disinterest or indifference, neither displaying much support for the current government nor going beyond mild declarations about appropriate domestic governance (i.e., a policy close to the status quo)?

   D. By encouraging European allies to take principal responsibility for adopting and managing an effective policy toward Turkey?

MEMORANDUM FOR THE PRESIDENT

From: Richard Burt

**Subject: What about Turkey Should (or Shouldn't)
         Concern You**

You have asked us for our views on U.S. interests in Turkey and concerns over developments there. In this memorandum, we will discuss (1) the strategic importance of Turkey to the United States and its allies and friends, and (2) the key issues and problems now confronting Turkey. In a companion memo, we briefly lay out and discuss U.S. policy options vis-à-vis Turkey.

TURKEY'S STRATEGIC IMPORTANCE

Turkey has long been strategically significant to the United States and the West as a whole. While located on the southeastern periphery of Europe, Turkey's forerunner entity, the Ottoman Empire, was periodically an important factor in 19th-century European great-power politics. For the United States, however, Turkey emerged as a key strategic factor in the early days of the Cold War, when Joseph Stalin's efforts to pressure Ankara into an accommodation highlighted, for the Truman administration, Turkey's geopolitical position between Europe and Central Asia. With its control of the strategic "choke point" between the Black Sea and the Mediterranean, its border with the southern republics of the Soviet Union, and its proximity to the Middle East, Turkey emerged as a natural bulwark against Soviet expansionism in the 1950s. Because of Turkey's historical anti-Russian and anti-Soviet orientation, its large and well-motivated army, and its willingness to cooperate closely with Washington (e.g. Jupiter IRBM deployments and U-2 basing and support), the country served as the linchpin of NATO's "southern flank" for more than 40 years. Although Washington and Ankara experienced a range of bilateral differences over such issues as Turkey's continuing differences with Greece and its human rights practices internally, the shared strategic imperative of deterring Soviet political-military pressure dissuaded either side from letting these issues dominate the relationship. Indeed, the shared management of the U.S.-Turkish relationship was one of more unsung accomplishments of this period.

With the collapse of the Soviet Union and the end of the Cold War, Turkey is one of the few states that, for the United States, has taken on greater—rather than less—strategic significance. Of course, while the Soviet Union is gone, Russia continues to possess important interests in southcentral Asia, although for now it does not possess the political or military power to pursue them in an aggressive, focused way. More importantly, Turkey—geographically, economically, and culturally—stands astride three zones of growing strategic importance to the United States:

1. The Middle East and the Gulf

Bordering Iran, Iraq, and Syria, Turkey's continued strength and stability—and its continued alliance with the United States—is a clear force for moderation and stability in the region as a whole. As the Gulf war and its aftermath vividly illustrated, Turkey is an essential partner for the projection of large-scale American power to the region. In view of reductions in U.S. force structure and political developments in the region, in any future Gulf contingency, particularly a conflict involving Iran, Turkey would play an even more important role. The same is true in the case of the Arab-Israeli dispute. Turkey's differences with Iraq, and to a lesser extent, Syria, make it more difficult for both to focus their energies in a campaign directed against Israel, a strategic fact that has led Tel Aviv to seek closer ties and cooperation with Ankara.

2. The Caucasus and Central Asia

The collapse of the Soviet Union has both liberated the energies of the former Soviet republics and created new opportunities in these regions for competition and conflict. This is particularly the case for the Caspian Sea Basin, which promises, in the coming decade, to become the world's second or third largest exporter of oil and natural gas. Turkey has emerged as an important player in this region, both as an economic partner and as a secure terminus for newly developed energy networks. In this role, Turkey, which is often allied with U.S. oil companies, often finds itself competing head-to-head with Russia and Iran for political access and economic influence.

3. Southeastern Europe

Turkey, of course, through NATO and a variety of other institutions, enjoys long-standing ties with Europe and is anxious to strengthen them (see below). In particular, since the end of the Cold War, Turkey has gradually built up its contacts in southeastern Europe, which remains the continent's most unstable and volatile region. Turkey is participating in the Stabilisation Force (SFOR) deployments in Bosnia, where its position as NATO's only "Islamic member" has given it special credibility. More importantly, its participation in the Black Sea Forum have strengthened ties with Ukraine and Romania, two states in which the United States has a deep interest in continuing political and economic reform.

Needless to say, Turkey's growing regional role has exposed it to a range of new threats. This is particularly true in the case for Turkey's Islamic neighbors, Iran, Iraq, and Syria. In some respects, Turkey is coming to occupy a role similar to that played by West Germany during the Cold War. Just as West Germany was Moscow's principal political-military target in the postwar era, Turkey has now become the key "front line" state in confronting the dominant dangers of the post-Cold War period: (1) nuclear proliferation (in the form of Iran and Iraq's efforts to build or obtain weapons of mass destruction); (2) terrorism (as embodied by the guerrilla war being waged by the Kurdish Nationalist Workers Party, the PKK, on Turkey's southeastern border with Iraq); and (3) radical Islamic fundamentalism (as practiced by Iran and by a variety of extremist groups active within Turkey, but *not* by the country's mainstream Islamic party, the Refah).

If Turkey's ties to the West and the United States, in particular, are preserved, then it should be possible for Turkey—working together with its allies—to stand up to these threats. Certainly, it is the desire and will of the current Turkish establishment, especially the military, to do so. But if, for a variety of mainly internal problems, the country's leadership loses the strong sense of will and direction that it has demonstrated since the Turkish Republic was founded in 1923 by Kemal Ataturk, the consequences for the United States could be enormous. Turkey, since the late 1940s, has been a strong and loyal U.S. ally which, from the Korean conflict through the Gulf war and beyond, has demonstrated a willingness to work closely with Washington to secure Western interests. A weakened, disintegrating Turkey, on the one hand, or a radicalized, hostile Turkey on the other, would not only deprive the United States of a strong partner uniquely positioned in a zone of growing importance. "Losing" Turkey would mean losing a democratic, pro-Western, Islamic role model in the region; a force for moderation and free-market development in the Caspian, the Caucasus, and beyond; a potential balancer in the Arab-Israeli dispute; and a force for stability in southeastern Europe.

TURKEY'S INTERNAL PROBLEMS

Turkey's complex and difficult strategic situation has historically provided a rationale for close links with Washington. Living as it does in arguably the world's toughest neighborhood, it is not surprising that Turkey seeks a strategic relationship with the world's only superpower. Internally, however, Turkey now faces a series of issues that threaten its political and social cohesion, and also place obstacles in the way of efforts by the United States and our European partners to cooperate more closely with the Turkish leadership. This is the dilemma of U.S.-Turkish relations.

In describing these issues, we will not attempt to analyze them exhaustively nor to propose solutions. Instead, we will try to distinguish among those trends in Turkey that should concern us and those that should not.

The first issue of real concern is the growth of the Islamic political movement and its escalating conflict with secular traditions and institutions of Turkish government. Of course, there has long been a latent conflict between Turkey's secular state and its Islamic culture. However, that conflict became real last year when, following elections, Necmettin Erbakan's Refah party found itself the largest political grouping in parliament. After forming a coalition government, Erbakan visited several radical Arab states and launched a fairly mild program of legitimizing Islamic practices in Turkey's schools, government bureaucracies, and military. After very visible signs of displeasure with Erbakan's program on the part of the Turkish military early this year, the coalition government led by the Refah fell in July. The beneficiary of the military's intervention, Mesut Yilmaz of the Motherland party, was then able to form a rickety coalition government. A new national election could occur over the next six months or so.

The drama raises two important questions for the future of the Refah and the Islamic movement in Turkey more generally. The first is the short-term question of how all of this is likely to affect the electoral prospects of the Refah in the coming election. While the military retains a role of great popular respect, will support for the Refah continue to grow as a result of Erbakan being forced out of office? A longer-term and more fundamental question has to do with the ultimate objectives of the Refah: is the movement prepared to coexist and even support the secularist principles laid down by Ataturk, or do its leaders cling to a more radical, even Iranian-style vision? Here, the experts disagree, with some arguing that the eventual goal of the Refah is the total overthrow of the secular establishment in Turkey, and others insisting that it has embraced modernism and can be co-opted into the country's leadership. Whatever the answer (and there may not be one at this point), the conflict between the legacy of Ataturk and the growing Islamic revival in Turkey is likely to grow in coming years, with important implications for the U.S.-Turkish relationship.

The second, related problem has to do with the role of the Turkish military. As this year's events vividly underscored, the place of the military in Turkish society differs qualitatively from the Western European and American experience. Since the founding of modern Turkey in 1923, the military has been closely connected to the Turkish concept of statehood. Since that time, six of Turkey's nine presidents have been former generals, and in the past 40 years, the military has actually taken power three times. (In each case, this was for a brief period and was triggered by clear signs of civilian political paralysis. Thus, it would be naïve and simplistic to ask whether the time has come for the generals—and the Turkish political system more broadly—to adopt an American-style practice of civilian control of the military. This is not in the cards, nor would it be necessarily desirable. The right question is whether, in light of current social trends in Turkish society, the military possesses the skill and adroitness to exercise its behind-the-scenes influence in a way that maintains national stability and cohesion. On this, the jury is out.

The third area of concern is Turkey's political leadership, particularly its ability to adjust the Turkish economy to the realities of a more competitive, globalized economy. Although the U.S. Commerce Department has anointed Turkey as one of its "big ten" emerging markets, its economic performance during the last decade has been disappointing. The main reason for this has been the failure of recent Turkish governments to curb inflation and to open the economy to free-market forces. For a brief period in the 1980s, Turkey's Prime Minister and then President Turgut Özal launched an important program of liberalization designed to cut government spending, to reduce state ownership and subsidies to key industrial sectors, and to create new incentives for private enterprise. The Özal reforms were successful in creating a new class of entrepreneurs that has continued to prosper into the 1990s. But many of Özal's efforts to restructure the Turkish economy, particularly those focused on reducing spending for state-supported enterprises, fell by the wayside under the timid, inept, and corrupt leadership of Prime Minister Tansu Ciller. The question now is whether the new Yilmaz government is prepared to relaunch the Özal reform program. This appears unlikely, given the pain that economic restructuring would entail and the fact that new elections probably lie just around the corner. Yet the failure of Turkish secular parties to take bold steps on the economy is likely to both boost popular support for Refah and confirm perceptions on the part of the Turkish military that the political leadership is incapable of addressing the country's real challenges.

While addressing the problems of Turkey that should greatly concern us, it is also important to note those that should not. There are two that bear mention. The first is Turkey's human rights record. Needless to say, facing various terrorist threats from abroad and radical extremism at home, Turkey's human rights practices are unlikely to ever pass muster with the Green party in Germany or the U.S. State Department's Bureau of Human Rights and Humanitarian Affairs. There is a pattern of human rights abuses in Turkey, particularly directed against the Kurdish minorities. That said, despite well-publicized campaigns by Turkey's critics in the West, Turkey's performance in this area has steadily improved. During the last two years, Turkey has taken a number of steps to demonstrate its responsiveness to Western concerns, including the establishment of a governmental human rights organization, passing new laws to protect civil liberties, and retraining police. In this regard, special note should be taken of the criticism often targeted on Turkey's prosecution of its military campaign in southeastern Turkey against the PKK. While it has recently adopted Islamic camouflage, the PKK is a militant, communist group of Kurdish terrorists whose avowed aim is not to achieve some form of political autonomy, but to establish a separate state on Turkish soil. (In this regard, it is also worth noting that in June 1997 the PKK announced that the group was prepared to target not only Turkish nationals, but also American and Israeli citizens.)

The second issue that should not weigh heavily in our thinking about Turkey is its long, drawn-out dispute with Greece. While this constellation of problems Cyprus, air and sea demarcation in the Aegean, and military exercises—loom large in Greek politics and for supporters of Greece in the United States, it is not a first-order security concern in Ankara. With U.S. and European prodding, both sides have recently demonstrated a tentative willingness to address their outstanding problems. But the probability of a real breakthrough, particularly concerning Cyprus, remains low. At the same time, however, the appetite for conflict on both sides has lessened. Increasingly, in the case of Greek-Turkish differences, form seems to matter more than substance.

Turkey's strategic importance to the United States is large, and is growing. The country's external posture has been, and remains, mostly in alignment with U.S. interests. However, a cluster of interrelated internal problems raises real questions about Turkey's willingness and capacity in the future to continue to play this role. These raise real dilemmas for U.S. policy, which are examined in a companion memo.

MEMORANDUM FOR THE PRESIDENT

From: Heath Lowry
Subject: How Turkish Leaders View America and
         the World

To answer the query implicit in this topic we must begin by coming to grips with the changing nature of political leadership in Turkey. The hypothesis I will advance herein is that in the past six months the political configuration in Turkey has undergone a gradual transformation from a traditional Western European-style parliamentary democracy to one in which decision-making on key issues has been increasingly assumed by the Turkish National Security Council (NSC), whose role has been superimposed over the existing and still-functioning governmental apparatus. Policies developed within the Turkish General Staff's 'Western Working Group' (WWG) are presented at regularly scheduled meetings of the NSC to elected policy officials for their agreement. This has occurred with the open support of a heretofore unseen coalition of elite groups (including labor unions, industrialists, the United Chambers of Commerce, university presidents, mainstream media, the intelligentsia, and, most importantly, the military), who were convinced that the basic tenet of "secularism" which underlies the Turkish state was threatened by the increasing power of Islamic fundamentalism as embodied in the *Refah Partisi* (the Prosperity or Welfare party) of Necmettin Erbakan. At present, overall policy (domestic and foreign) in Turkey is being determined by the president (Süleyman Demirel), the prime minister (Mesut Yilmaz), and the chief of the Turkish general staff (İsmail Karadayi), on behalf of the country's constitutionally powerful NSC. To comprehend what has led to this situation we must briefly review events of the past 12 months:

- In June of 1996 a coalition government led by Necmettin Erbakan (the head of the avowedly Islamist Refah party, which had emerged as the chief vote-getter in the December 1995 general elections, with 21.3 percent of the electorate's support), and Tansu Ciller (the leader of the presumably Western-oriented, secular *Dogru Yol Partisi*—"True Path party" or DYP), was formed. To say that this was a marriage of convenience is an understatement. Ciller had run her December 1995 election campaign on the promise that she and she alone could halt the growing strain of religious fundamentalism represented by *Refah* in Turkey, thereby ensuring Turkey's ultimate integration into the EU; whereas Erbakan's campaign had included a pledge to bring Ciller (and her spouse Özer) before the tribune of justice to account for a series of well-based charges of corruption stemming from her earlier stint as prime minister. Six months later Ciller climbed into bed with Islam and promptly shed her Western mantle and Erbakan began blocking all attempts to investigate the past activities of the Ciller family.

- For six months the *Refah-Yol* (Prosperity Path) coalition, with Erbakan as prime minister and Ciller as deputy prime minister and minister of foreign affairs, stumbled along from self-imposed crisis to crisis (several precipitated in the course of Erbakan's visits to one or another extremist Islamic state). Its most notable achievements were the printing of currency and the staffing of the state payrolls with more than 60,000 Refah party loyalists (two activities they had learned from their predecessors).

- Statements by various Refah spokesmen convinced a wide spectrum of groups within the country's traditional ruling elite that despite Erbakan's lip service in support of democracy, his party's real goal was the implementation of an Islamic regime in Turkey—stated differently, that Erbakan and company were simply using democracy as a tool to implement an agenda which would ultimately destroy it. This elite perception was heightened by a feeling that Tansu Ciller (whom many of the elite had supported) had betrayed the country by joining forces with Erbakan, and therefore that Refah (which only represented 20 percent of the electorate), was attempting to dictate a new political system for the majority 80 percent who had not supported it in the December 1995 elections. In the ensuing months public opposition to the *Refah-Yol* coalition began to coalesce to the extent that even traditional enemies, such as the country's two major labor confederations, joined forces calling for an end to the Erbakan-Ciller government.

- The first real crack in the facade of normalcy occurred in November 1996, when a fatal car crash in the town of Susurluk gave credence to charges already circulating in the press that there was a coalition of evil represented by security forces run amok, former right-wing terrorists now operating as government-sanctioned death squads cum narcotic smugglers, progovernment Kurdish tribal leaders, all under the control of one of Ciller's closest associates, Mehmet Agar, a former head of security and minister of justice, who was currently serving as a DYP deputy and minister of the interior. In the ensuing months as the investigation moved haltingly forward, it became increasingly apparent that little more than the tip of a largely submerged iceberg had emerged. Lurking below the surface was the always present Özer Ciller, the spouse of Tansu. Here too, efforts to investigate were thwarted by the government.

- Throughout this period the extremist wing of Refah continued flexing its muscle and Erbakan (presumably to keep control over his disparate forces), engaged in a series of highly publicized events designed to please his adherents—most notably the hosting of a Ramazan *İftar* (fast-breaking) dinner, in honor of a number of leaders of *Derviş* religious orders (*Tarikats*) and other extremist religious factions, which was held in the prime minister's official residence.

- On February 28, 1997, Turkey experienced (what time would show was) its fourth military coup d'état in the past 40 years. Unlike its predecessors, this one did not involve the movement of troops into the streets, the declaring of martial law and the open assumption of civilian power by the armed forces. Unique in style (it had the more than tacit support of all facets of Turkey's traditional ruling elite), this coup may best be labeled a "soft coup": a coup by "demands" issued by the National Security Council (a military/civilian body with broad constitutional powers to "preserve the peace and security of society" and the "independence of the state"). It took the form of issuing a list of some 18 steps which the government must implement. While both Erbakan and Ciller, as members of the NSC, affixed their signatures to the "demands," it soon became clear that Erbakan had no intention of actually implementing them. By openly stating that these demands were nonnegotiable, the NSC set into motion the series of events which were to bring the *Refah-Yol* government down some four months later.

- While one may debate whether or not demands such as the strict enforcement of laws implemented in the 1920s designed to regulate the wearing of religious apparel in public actually fall under the NSC's constitutional mandate of preserving the peace and security of society or the independence of the state, the fact that the military's goals were shared by the media, the leading business associations, labor unions, university presidents, the intelligentsia and others created a climate wherein they enjoyed widespread public support, i.e., there was no public outcry that the NSC was stretching its mandate.

- While most of these demands were designed to buttress the traditional Ataturkist secular state against the perceived inroads of fundamentalist Islam, subsequent events were to demonstrate that it was what at first glance appeared to be one of the more innocuous demands which would prove to be the most controversial. Namely, a statement that "eight years of unbroken education should be implemented throughout the country." (Mandatory schooling now stands at five years.) Viewed by fundamentalists as an attempt to curb their primary breeding grounds, the *İmam-Hatip* schools (schools for the training of religious functionaries) provide a growing cadre of educated Muslims, the overwhelming proportion of whom find their way not into religious oriented occupations, but rather into one or another branch of the state bureaucracy (in particular the ministries of education, justice and the interior; i.e., they become the nation's schoolteachers, prosecutors, judges, police and provincial governors).

- Given the failure of either Erbakan and Ciller to implement the NSC demands they had signed under pressure, the military's newly-formed antifundamentalist Western Working Group (WWG) began to up the ante by going public in late May with a series of briefings presented to various segments of the Turkish ruling elite, such as jurists, diplomats, businessmen and journalists. While Refah was never specifically mentioned in these briefings, their content was primarily comprised of film depicting the fundamentalist activities of Refah politicians.

- Simultaneously, an anti-Refah media campaign orchestrated by the chief of staff's Western Working Group went into effect: major print and electronic media outlets were provided copies of clandestinely-shot film footage depicting Refah politicians making strong anti-secularist and profundamentalist speeches. The fact that much of this footage dated from the early 1990s did not deter either the media or the Turkish elite. A mounting crescendo of prosecularist (anti-Refah) rhetoric began to resonate in all the organs which traditionally shape Turkish public opinion.

- Likewise the general staff's spokesman leaked the names of a series of what were deemed to be pro-Refah business corporations and announced that in the future the Turkish military would do no business with any of them.

- The ante was raised when the chief of the general staff's spokesman went public with an announcement that henceforth the number one enemy of the state was *İrtica,* meaning reactionaryism, meaning fundamentalism; that *İrtica* represented an even greater threat to Turkey than did the PKK (the Kurdish insurgency movement); and that the same diligence with which the armed forces were striving to eliminate the danger represented by the PKK would now be directed against the danger represented by *İrtica.* Implicit in this announcement was the message that in the minds of the military, Refah equaled *İrtica,* and that the party's continued role in government was perceived as a threat to the survival of the state.

- By early June the campaign was in full swing; events had progressed to the point that prosecutors had brought a still-pending case calling for the banning of Refah before the Constitutional Court) and Necmettin Erbakan, realizing that he no longer could control events, determined on a desperate gamble and agreed that he would be replaced by Tansu Ciller as Prime Minister, i.e., that what had been the Prosperity Path coalition (*Refah-Yol*) would now become the Path [to] Prosperity coalition (*Yol-Refah*). To do so he had to submit the resignation of his government to President Demirel and then assume that Demirel would ask Tansu Ciller to form a new government. To make sure that Demirel understood the proposed mathematics, the members of Refah and DYP signed an agreement that they would support the proposed Ciller-Erbakan government. Stated differently, Erbakan assumed (incorrectly as subsequent events would prove) that Demirel would have no choice but to turn to Ciller given the fact that the combined vote of the two parties ensured a successful vote of confidence in Parliament.

- The miscalculation of Erbakan and Ciller appears in retrospect to have stemmed from the fact that Ciller (once the darling of the military) assumed that the general staff's unhappiness would dissipate were she to become prime minister. This miscalculation bears out the Turkish proverb *Evdeki hesap çarsiya uymaz,* or, "the accounting one makes at home doesn't fit the prices in the marketplace." In short, their reasoning failed to take into account the nature of the military opposition or the extent to which President Demirel had bought into the Refah threat-perception scenario laid out by the general staff.

- Demirel, without hesitation, turned not to Tansu Ciller, but rather to Mesut Yilmaz, chairman of the Motherland party (*Anavatan Partisi,* or ANAP), i.e., the party of the late Turgut Özal, and asked him to form a government. Given the mathematics involved this appeared to be an impossible task, particularly when the members of both Erbakan and Ciller's parties immediately signed a declaration stating that they would not give a vote of confidence to a Yilmaz government. Here too, the role of Demirel was important: indications are that he began pressuring a number of Ciller's deputies (the True Path party was the creation of Demirel, and Ciller only came to power in the political vacuum created by his leaving its leadership to assume the presidency in 1993 following the death of Özal), urging them to resign their party memberships and support the Yilmaz coalition. Breakaway DYP forces began trying to pressure other of their colleagues to join them in forming a new parliamentary group and the defections continued.

- By July 1, 1997, Yilmaz had announced the formation of a new governing coalition comprising ANAP, the Democratic Left party (DSP) of Bülent Ecevit, the Democratic Turkey party (DTP) of Ismet Sezgin and Hüsamettin Cindoruk (the new parliamentary group formed by breakaway members of Ciller's DYP), and an assortment of independent deputies. While not represented in the governing coalition, the Republic People's party (CHP) of Deniz Baykal announced that it too would support the Yilmaz coalition by giving it their vote of confidence. Two weeks later the Turkish Republic's 55th government received a vote of confidence (with a majority of 25 out of 550 parliamentary votes).

- In the ensuing weeks both Erbakan and Ciller cried foul play, claiming that votes were purchased and that this is really not the Yilmaz government, but rather that of President Demirel and the military, and so forth. Partly in response to their unveiled attacks on the person of the president, defections from both DYP and Refah continue to add to the ranks of the Yilmaz ruling coalition.

- On at least one occasion in recent weeks, Prime Minister Yilmaz, President Demirel, and Chief of Staff Karadayi met together in a strategy session which had the effect of sending a clear signal that Turkey is currently ruled by not one but two coalitions: (1) the leaders of the National Security Council form one tier, and (2) the Yilmaz coalition (ANAP, DSP, DTP, independents, and the tacit support of the CHP), i.e., the parliament and council of ministers, which comprise the traditional civilian parliamentary system, form a second tier.

- Unable or unwilling to accept this political reality, Refah has begun to challenge the status-quo ante "soft coup" by signaling its supporters (via their wing of the print and electronic media) that it is time to address their grievances in the street. Their rallying cry is opposition to the new government's intention to go ahead with implementing mandatory eight-year education, a step that Refah partisans are convinced is designed to destroy their breeding grounds, the *İmam-Hatip* (religious) school system. While to date these efforts have resulted in no mass outpourings, a rally on July

31, 1997, in the capital of Ankara did draw some 4,000 fundamentalists. More disturbing was the reaction of the police who while protecting the demonstrators mishandled rather brutally a number of journalists covering the event. When it turned out that the police tapes of the rally mysteriously had been cleansed of evidence of police brutality, the press provided the necessary footage. In the ensuing investigation, policemen queried as to why they did not disperse the illegal demonstration and instead went after the journalists stated: "They [the demonstrators] are our mothers and fathers who share our views. It is the press who are our enemies." While 4,000 demonstrators in 1997 Ankara are a far cry from the hundreds of thousands who flooded the streets of 1979 Tehran, early signs that some members of the security forces are beginning to identify with the Islamists rather than with the state should not be overlooked. The fact is that such Refah efforts go a long way toward reinforcing the military's belief (clearly stated in the NSC's February 28, 1997, list of demands) that it is the Iranian Revolution which serves as the model for their real intentions.

It is against this background that we must return to the query this paper is intended to address: How do Turkish political figures see their world (and us)?" To the extent the proceeding analysis has succeeded, it should be clear that its author views Turkey as currently in a state of limbo. On the one hand, all the trappings of its constitutionally ordained parliamentary system (albeit somewhat battered) remain in place; there is a civilian government and therefore we may discuss Turkish political leaders and their world views. On the other hand, there is (as the result of what I have termed the soft coup) a kind of shadow government comprising key members of the NSC (the president, the prime minister, the chief of the Turkish general staff) who determine both domestic and foreign policy and consequently influence the parliamentary agenda as well.

CONCLUSION

For the past 12 months Turkey's political leaders have increasingly come to view their world in terms of a Huntingtonian model and themselves as engaged in the "clash of civilizations" he forecasts. They see the West (which all with the exception of Erbakan intuitively know they are part of) as arrayed against the forces of Islam represented by the Refah party. Erbakan likewise shares this view of the world with the only difference being that he sees Turkey as belonging in the Islamic camp. To the extent that the West is equated in the minds of all with the United States, Turkish political leaders (again with the exception of Erbakan), are all willing for even closer cooperation with us. In particular, the present Yilmaz coalition government has signaled its willingness for increased cooperation with the United States on a variety of issues.

Somewhat paradoxically, at the very time the West is increasingly focused on Turkey's still unresolved Kurdish problem, the Turkish military (and Turkish public opinion) has shifted its primary focus to the secularist struggle. This fact is clearly reflected in the Turkish media, which, aside from daily "body counts," largely ignore the ongoing Kurdish conflict in favor of following the *İrtica* debate. Stated differently, it appears that the military's attempts to define the Kurdish insurgency as primarily a "terrorist problem," which they are capable of defeating, has been accepted by the Turkish public at large. This shortsighted view does not bode well for Turkey's ability to meaningfully address the underlying discontent of a significant portion of its Kurdish citizenry, which fuels the PKK (Kurdish Nationalist Workers party) movement.

This is the game as it appears on August 1, 1997, and these are the players in it. Will the current coalition government hold at least until it achieves its initial goal of updating voting registers by carrying out a nationwide census (tentatively scheduled for later this year), and setting the ground rules for parliamentary elections to be held sometime in the next two years? I would venture a hesitant yes to this query. Not because one should trust the various parties (and their leaders) presently represented in parliament, but rather because it appears that the first tier of state power wants this to happen. Will Refah be represented in the parties vying for votes in 1998? Probably not (at least under its current name and present leadership), and for the same reasons. Will the current impasse and voter fragmentation—no party received more than 21 percent of the vote in the last general elections—be resolved as a result of the soft coup engineered by what I have termed the first tier of state authority? Almost certainly not, unless the mainstream center-right and center-left parties find a way of setting aside their differences and forming single parties with which a larger percentage of the voters can identify.

The great unknown in this equation is the future role of the Turkish general staff (TGS) in the country's domestic political agenda. On August 1, 1997, the Turkish press reported on a top secret report prepared by the Western Working Group, in which it was stressed that:

> "the power of religious organizations, due to years of governmental indifference, had grown to the point that the forces who seek a return of the *İeriat* (Islamic religious law) system in Turkey had managed to take over key governmental agencies. Further, that if steps to the contrary were not taken, it is possible that the fundamentalists' political wing [note: read Refah] could come to power by itself in the year 2000."

Clearly, this is something the TGS will not tolerate, and it goes a long way toward explaining the reasoning behind their actions in recent months. In short, the TGS's view of their world and us (the United States) is closely related to its perceived security threats. Our continued overt support is essential for their goal of suppressing the Kurdish terrorist movement, and our tacit acceptance facilitates the goals of the current soft coup against the danger of fundamentalism. Despite all protestations to the contrary, the TGS via its chief of staff and the National Security Council, is and will remain for the foreseeable future a key player in the political life of Turkey.

Finally, will Mesut Yilmaz be able to gain sufficient credibility with the TGS to force the disbanding of its WWG, i.e. to get the army to return to its barracks as far as the fight against reactionaryism is concerned? Here only time will tell. However, early indications suggest that the TGS is totally committed (at least under the present leadership configuration) to waging war against what it sees as antisecularist forces. Should its moves against Refah be followed by similar steps intended to enforce the 18 points set forth in the NSC's February 28, 1997, demands, this analysis will be borne out.

MEMORANDUM FOR THE PRESIDENT

From: Richard Burt

**Subject: Critical Strategic Choices in U.S. Policy
           toward Turkey**

In my preceding memo, it was concluded that it is an important U.S.
interest to preserve its long-standing political-military partnership with
Turkey. It was also underscored, however, that internal developments
in Turkey will make this increasingly difficult to do. In this memo,
three broad options will be described and analyzed for how the United
States could address this important but complex task.

THE CURRENT APPROACH

The first option would be to essentially stick to the current policy. This
would mean that the administration would continue to offer strong
rhetorical support for Ankara's pro-Western orientation, but would exercise restraint and caution in actual dealings with the Turkish leadership.

As the analysis in my first memo suggests, a continuation of the status
quo approach to Turkey is unlikely to succeed. So far, at any rate, it has
not contributed to a lessening of the internal contradictions in Turkish
society. At the same time, the current policy has led many of America's
staunchest supporters in the Turkish leadership to question
Washington's real commitment to Turkey. This is not surprising,
because the administration's current approach is more a product of top-
level neglect than strategic design. In the absence of high-level interest
in Turkey on the part of the U.S. national security apparatus (the
National Security Council, the State and Defense departments, and the
intelligence community), Turkish policy has become a hostage to special interests in the bureaucracy, outside lobby groups, and political
advocacy in the Congress.

The result of high-level inattention to Turkey has created an approach
to Turkey that is neither coherent nor consistent. For example, while
U.S. spokesmen have repeatedly stressed Turkey's strategic importance as an ally, the administration's decisions concerning Turkish

arms sales requests suggest otherwise. Until very recently, the administration has applied a de facto embargo on the sale of all major military items to the Turkish military. This includes the transfer of naval frigates, attack helicopters, antiterrorist equipment, and even tear gas. In the case of the frigates, deliveries were held up for more than two years despite personal assurances given to President Süleyman Demirel in the White House that their transfer was imminent. (The administration has finally agreed to notify Congress of the release of the warships following an agreement by the foreign ministers of Turkey and Greece in July in Madrid covering "a convergence of views on a basis for promoting better relations" facilitated by Secretary of State Albright.)

There are several disturbing aspects of the administration's performance on arms sales that transcend the technical-military issues at stake. First, the administration's slowdown and/or embargo on military sales has been essentially justified on grounds that have little or nothing to do with any objective assessment of threats facing Turkey. In fact, I am not aware of any analysis done in the Pentagon or elsewhere that suggests that Turkey does not need to modernize its forces. Instead, the embargo has been justified by U.S. officials based on two factors: the continuing problem of human rights in Turkey, and congressional opposition to new sales, particularly on the part of supporters of Greece. As we have seen, there is not a strong basis for permitting either human rights or the Greek-Turkish problem to drive U.S. policy toward Turkey. In the case of human rights, we have already noted that Ankara's performance in this area is improving. Equally important, it is hard to understand how curtailing arms deliveries will improve the situation further. The Turks are not requesting equipment, such as stealth aircraft, than can only be procured from the United States. The world arms export market has grown more open and more competitive, and Turkey can meet most of its military requirements from other suppliers, particularly France and Russia. The question thus emerges: Will Turkey have greater incentives to exercise restraint in the use of force if it buys its arms from France and Russia than it would if it continued to rely on the United States?

As for the Greek-Turkish dispute, we have already seen that this dispute, while troublesome, is unlikely to threaten fundamental U.S. interests in the region. More importantly, the argument that a U.S. arms blockade will somehow enhance prospects for a settlement in the Aegean is highly suspect. Since the Turkish invasion of Cyprus in 1974, it has become abundantly clear that any effort to coerce Turkey to the bargaining table is destined to fail. Indeed, what little progress that has been made in resolving the Greek-Turkish tangle has occurred when both parties have felt more, rather than less, secure. Moreover, the idea that Turkey alone holds the key to peace is itself spurious: any real settlement will require concessions from both sides.

Another disturbing aspect of the administration's approach to arms sales is the impact it is likely to have on the Turkish military, a central player in the country's external and internal affairs. The Turkish military has, for 40 years, based its force structure and operational planning on U.S. equipment and plans. In wartime, Turkish forces pledged to NATO would come under the command of a senior U.S. officer. This organic military linkage has undoubtedly been beneficial to the United States in several ways. For a start, the "special relationship" between the U.S. and Turkish military has provided the current and previous administrations with a privileged channel of communications to a powerful, but hidden actor in Turkish politics. The U.S.-Turkish military link has also been important in winning Turkish support for risky and controversial commitments, such as its support for coalition activities during Desert Storm, its cooperation in Operation Northern Shield in Iraq, and its deployments in Bosnia. The close linkage between the U.S. and Turkish militaries has undoubtedly provided Washington with unspoken leverage over both military and civilian leaders in Ankara. Thus, when U.S.-Turkish military ties are threatened, so is American influence more generally, including in such areas as human rights, relations with Greece, and NATO issues more broadly.

Finally, the arms sales issue reinforces for the Turkish leadership the perception that Turkey is not a major foreign policy priority of the administration. The argument that the administration cannot make good on promised arms deliveries leaves Turkish officials bewildered, because they have seen on issues such as NAFTA, MFN for China, and now NATO expansion how the administration has been able to effectively counter congressional opposition. In the case of Turkey, however, Cabinet-level officials have generally remained detached from issues of central importance to Ankara, with the result that Turkish policy has been thrown into the Washington political "bazaar," where middle-level bureaucrats, congressional staffers, NGOs, and special interest groups engage in an endless round of horse-trading on second-order issues. The end result is drift and stalemate.

Clearly then, the administration's current policy of supporting Turkey publicly but then failing to follow through with specific actions is not a viable course for the future. A policy of detached, or distanced, support will not in the long run secure U.S. interests in Turkey. In fact, it risks doing just the opposite.

THE EUROPEAN OPTION

An alternative to the existing policy would be to ask the Europeans to take the lead in supporting Turkey's security needs and coping with its political and economic problems. Under this option, the administration would press its NATO allies and the European Union to launch a series of programs to move Turkey closer to Europe, including membership in the EU. Under such a policy, the United States would seek to maintain a healthy bilateral relationship with Ankara, but avoid the risks and complications associated with serving as Turkey's chief strategic partner.

There are clear advantages for both the United States and Turkey of greater Turkish-European engagement. Europe, like the United States, has a major stake in Turkey's strategic role, and Ankara has long sought closer political-economic ties with Europe. But the idea that Europe could substitute for the U.S. role in Turkey is flawed. To begin with, Turkey's recent efforts to move closer to Europe have, in many cases, been rebuffed. Turkey was finally able last year to join the European Customs Union, but only after a drawn-out and humiliating debate which focused on its human rights record. Particularly in northern Europe, there are deep-seated cultural concerns about moving closer to Turkey's Islamic society, particularly the possibility that this could lead to increased immigration and potential social problems. (In Germany, for example, Turkish *gastarbeiters* have lived and worked there for over 20 years and are still not permitted to apply for citizenship.) This pattern of xenophobia, together with strenuous Greek opposition, has blocked earnest efforts by the Turks to gain admission to the European Union. With Europeans focused on internal issues such as monetary union, as well as the challenges of bringing several Eastern Europeans into the union over the next few years, Turkish accession is unlikely to receive any serious attention for some time, if ever.

The same is true as regards European security and military cooperation with Turkey. Traditionally, the Turks have found themselves at odds with European defense planners over military strategy. This is because while Europeans focused on threats to northcentral Europe, the Turks, not surprisingly, worried about contingencies in their region. (This tension manifested itself very vividly during conventional force reduction negotiations in the early 1990s, when the Soviet Union sought to redeploy forces directed against central Europe to its southern military districts.) This tension has abated since the end of the Cold War, but as the debate over NATO expansion reveals, it still exists.

Yet there is a more fundamental problem in giving Europe the lead in managing Turkish security. Europe as a whole, and the EU in particular, lacks any concept or consensus over how to protect Western interests beyond its own borders. As the fiasco in Bosnia clearly underscored, even in Europe the capacity for designing and then executing coherent political-military strategy is woefully underdeveloped. In the Middle East, the Caspian Basin, and Central Asia, there is no such thing as a European security policy. While European governments and arms manufacturers would be happy to obtain the added revenues and jobs created by supplanting the United States as Turkey's major military supplier, the idea that Europe could replace the United States as Turkey's security partner is, bluntly put, a pipe dream.

Aggressive Engagement by the United States

This brings us to the third option, which is for the United States to adopt an aggressive and comprehensive program for strengthening its ties to Turkey. Such a program would require new initiatives in a number of areas as well as the exercise of restraint in others. But before this program is outlined, it is necessary to make an important point. A new effort to preserve and strengthen Turkey's current position will only have a chance to succeed if the administration is prepared to devote the energy, time, and resources necessary to engage with Turkey in a coherent and consistent manner. In other words, Turkey as an issue would have to be upgraded to the cabinet-level and become one of the administration's top four or five national security priorities. The new importance attached to Turkey will then need to be clearly communicated to the bureaucracy of the Congress.

A new U.S. policy of "aggressive engagement" should have four features:

1. The administration needs to reach out to Turkey, both politically and economically.

Even though current Turkish politics are in flux, the administration needs to show open, strong support for pro-Western political forces in Ankara, including the current Yilmaz government. However, this support should extend beyond political parties to reach opinion leaders in the media, academic commentators, and perhaps most importantly the Turkish military. At the same time, U.S. officials should not be afraid to engage with moderate Islamic political forces at work. The objective of U.S. political engagement should not be to isolate or discourage Islamic currents, but to help promote a setting in which Turkey's secular institutions can survive and prosper in an Islamic cultural context.

In some respects, the task confronting us is similar to challenges faced in U.S. diplomacy in postwar West Germany. In that situation, the United States clearly preferred the ascendancy of conservative, pro-NATO forces, such as the Christian Democrats. At the same time, it was recognized that it would be shortsighted and counterproductive to alienate the anti-NATO, socialist opposition in the Social Democratic Party (SPD). Thus, a broad-based program of contacts with all mainstream political forces was initiated, which included political dialogue, visits to the United States, exchange programs, and careful intelligence monitoring. The result was that by the time that the SPD took power in the 1970s, not only did the U.S. government enjoy the trust and confidence of most SPD leaders, but the party itself came over time to embrace consensus NATO views. A similar effort should be launched in Turkey. The administration needs to show clear support for its friends in Ankara, while just as clearly demonstrating its readiness to work with those who are skeptical of close U.S. ties. This will not be an easy task, and it will be made more difficult by increased polarization in Turkish politics and society. Thus, part of a new engagement policy should be to quietly encourage bridge-building and reconciliation between moderate secular and Islamic forces. The military obviously has an important role to play here and the administration must work harder to develop a special channel to the Turkish General Staff. The U.S. embassy in Ankara will need to strengthen both its political and its public affairs activities, and an ambassador with expertise, public stature, and strong ties to the White House should be put in place. Former Senator Sam Nunn would fit the bill perfectly.

It is more difficult for the administration to promote stronger economic links; these will be driven by multinational financial institutions and companies based largely on the condition of the Turkish economy. That said, the administration can help stimulate trade and investment. The Treasury and Commerce departments should be instructed to give Turkey priority in their international programs, and U.S. officials, together with private-sector leaders, need to work closely with Ankara to restart the Özal reforms of the 1980s. In addition, the administration, at the highest levels, should step up pressure on the Europeans concerning Turkey's push to enter the European Union. EU membership may not, in the end, be a realistic option. But the United States should press for the closest possible relationship with the EU. Perhaps most important in the near term would be a U.S. effort to ensure that Turkey shares in the emerging Caspian Sea oil bonanza. There are strong strategic and economic incentives for the United States to lobby hard for the proposed pipeline between Baku in Azerbaijan and the Turkish port of Ceyhan in the Mediterranean. (The alternative would be to build pipelines controlled by Russia and Iran.) The administration, together with U.S. oil companies, should also support the construction of new oil terminals on Turkey's Black Sea coast and the installation of modern navigation systems in the Turkish Straits to safely accommodate larger tankers.

2. A new policy toward Turkey would strengthen U.S.-Turkish military ties.

The most important step now would be to restart U.S. arms sales. Situated in a uniquely dangerous neighborhood, Turkey has defense needs that are large and legitimate. The administration should immediately grant Turkish requests to buy U.S. equipment that has been bottled up in the bureaucracy for years, including gear suited for combating terrorism. Over the longer term, it should be the aim of U.S. policy to facilitate arrangements for coproducing U.S. military equipment in Turkey, such as modern attack helicopters. This would not only strengthen Turkey's defense industrial base, but also repair somewhat frayed ties with the Turkish military.

3. A policy of bolstering Turkey should be distanced from its dispute with Greece over Cyprus and other Aegean issues.

It is of course not possible to totally divorce the two altogether. It is useful that the administration and the United Nations are taking new initiatives to seek a resolution of the problems in the Eastern Mediterranean. Progress in this area would reinforce efforts to strengthen and stabilize Turkey. But if these efforts do not pan out, the administration should not give Athens or the Greek lobby in Congress leverage to use the lack of progress on Cyprus or related issues as an excuse for continuing to try to isolate Turkey.

4. U.S. policy needs to keep the human rights issue in perspective.

Human rights are an important component of U.S. foreign policy. Thus, this subject should remain an element of the U.S.-Turkish dialogue. But we need to remember that Turkey has been—and remains—a loyal friend and a strategic ally. We also need to recognize that the Turks are taking steps to address this problem and that closer political, military, and economic links will encourage further progress.

Needless to say, the policy advocated here carries with it some risks. Any increase in the U.S. political and military commitment in this volatile region must be weighed carefully. It will have consequences for U.S. relations with Russia, the U.S. position in the Middle East, and developments in Iran and Iraq. Within Turkey, efforts to bridge the widening gap between Islam and secularism may not succeed; in that case, we will be forced to make some difficult choices. At home, assigning Turkey new priority will create problems on Capitol Hill and with special interests.

In the final analysis, however, the advantages of aggressive engagement far outweigh the possible risks. We are approaching a critical juncture in our relationship with Turkey's fundamental alignment at stake. One commentator in the *Wall Street Journal* put it well: "Losing Turkey would not only be a major political debacle for the Clinton Administration, but also a national security disaster for the United States."

MEMORANDUM FOR THE PRESIDENT

From: Heath Lowry

**Subject: Critical Strategic Choices in U.S. Policy
           toward Turkey**

If Richard Burt and Heath Lowry are asked to discuss critical strategic choices in U.S. policy toward Turkey, it seems logical to assume that the "U.S. policy" part of the equation falls to Burt and the "Turkey" to Lowry. Consequently, the following analysis is intended to present a view of the world as seen from Ankara. It is not intended to argue that this *weltanschauung* is: (1) one I share; or, (2) one which the United States can or should accept. Rather it is an attempt to consciously present a one-sided view of the equation. As such, it discusses: (1) the ongoing struggle between the secularists and Islamists in Turkey and its foreign policy implications; (2) the manner in which Turkish foreign policy is currently made and by whom; (3) the major complaints/concerns/problems as articulated to this writer by these players; and (4) the ideal resolution to these issues from the perspective of foreign policy makers in Ankara. It is not an attempt to defend these views nor to suggest that the world as seen from Ankara is one which the United States or any other nation can or should accept.

Basic to comprehending any policy choices facing the U.S. vis-à-vis Turkey at this juncture in history is an understanding of the battle which is currently raging for the hearts and minds of that country's citizenry. Here we see arrayed two clearly opposing ideologies: a nationalist perspective which views Turkey as an integral part of the Western world; and one which sees it as a country which must return to its Islamic roots. This struggle has in the past 12 months become an all-consuming one. It most clearly influences among other things the manner in which Turks view their relationship with the United States and with the world at large.

The first school is that of the traditional urban elite and comprises roughly 10 million of Turkey's 60-million-plus population. These are the true children and grandchildren of the Ataturk revolution and include the majority of the educated, the business community, the traditional state bureaucrats, and, most importantly, the military. They are staunchly secularist (most having been raised as semi-agnostics at best) and equate anything having to do with a political role for religion as a threat to the security of the state. These are the groups who, in principle, were tasked by Ataturk with carrying out the trickle-down theory of modernization and Westernization, i.e., those who were to spread the message of the revolution among their fellow citizens. While they themselves are westernized they have failed to instill the same value system in that portion of the population whose roots are in the small towns and countryside. Today, given the fact that the population explosion experienced by Turkey in the past two decades has disproportionately affected the rural population, the traditional elite is in one sense fighting a losing battle. Stated differently, the trickle-down has trickled to a halt and it is now the large numbers of rural people who have migrated to the urban centers—complete with their own value systems—who threaten the world of the elite.

Secularism never took deep root in the Turkish countryside. In particular, the more heterodox forms of Islam, represented by the Dervish religious orders, continued to hold sway among millions of rural Turks. While this has always been the situation in Turkey, until recently the urban elite blithely managed to pretend that they, and they alone, were Turkey. With the advent of mass rural-to-urban migration in the past few decades it is no longer possible for the urban elite to ignore the fact that their values are not shared by the majority of the population. For even the majority of the urban population today have a far different feeling toward the importance of Islam than that of the traditional elite.

Since the advent of multiparty democracy in Turkey (post-1950), politicians of all stripes have vied for the religious vote. In the 1950s it was the Democrat party of Adnan Menderes, in the 1960s and 1970s the Justice party of Süleyman Demirel, in the 1980s the ANAP of Turgut Özal, and in the 1990s Necmettin Erbakan's Refah, which have played the religious card most effectively in their efforts to gain the votes of this segment of the population. Step by step the strict, almost Jacobin, secularism of the early years of the republic has been eroded as more and more concessions have been made to religious sensitivities. In this sense, Refah is simply the logical conclusion of a process which had been proceeding apace for the last 50 years. The difference is that today the elite is face to face with the rapid "Anatolization" of its urban strongholds—Islam has come to the cities.

The most conservative of the protectors of Atatürk's secularist legacy have always been the Turkish military. Consequently, it is logical that it was the military who first sounded the alert as to the perceived danger of the Refah movement, nor is it strange that it was actions taken by the Turkish General Staff (TGS), via its Western Working Group (WWG), which ultimately caused the fall (at least temporarily) of Erbakan's government. In the same manner that they initially opposed his domestic policies, they likewise were extremely upset by his foreign policy, marked as it was by a deemphasizing of its traditional Western orientation and its rather clumsy attempts to forge new ties with the Islamic east.

If there has been a miscalculation in the military's thinking, it may well prove to have stemmed from its almost phobic fear and distrust of religion, i.e., its tendency to see the only cause for the electoral successes enjoyed by Refah in recent years as religion. But for many of the rural-to-urban immigrants, townspeople and villagers who support Refah do so not for its religious content alone but because they do not see the hope for a better economic future for themselves and their children in today's Turkey. Turkey's embracing of a free-market economy in the mid-1980s has led to chronic near-hyperinflation and a decreasing standard of living for millions of middle- and lower-class Turks. None of the mainstream center-left and center-right parties are effectively addressing the problems thus created. Refah is at least paying lip service to the concerns of those millions of Turks who see a few percent of their compatriots at the top of the pyramid doing very well indeed, while they are having trouble feeding themselves. When Erbakan holds forth the promise of an *adil düzen,* a "just system," it is only the elite (and the military in particular) who equate this solely with the reimposition of an Islamic legal system. For millions of Turks he is telling them that he realizes the injustices of the economic system they are living under and promising to address the problems it creates.

In short, Turkey is in a period of real transition. Either the elite will wake up to the reality of the problems caused by the growing economic gap between the haves and have-nots, as well as to the fact that it is well past time for a serious reexamination of some aspects of the Ataturk legacy (in particular its reliance on the military to emerge in moments of perceived crisis as a kind of deus ex machina—as well as its willingness to forget democracy and human rights at such times), or the forces that brought Refah to power in 1996 will continue to grow. There can be no doubt but that, given the present stance of the military, such a development might ultimately lead to a direct military intervention, notwithstanding U.S. pressure to the contrary.

It is against this background that a discussion of the Turkish perspective on its relations with the United States and with Europe and its neighbors must be based. For this exercise to be meaningful a brief overview of recent events affecting the Turkish foreign policy establishment is in order: From June 1996 to June 1997 the nominal minister of foreign affairs in Turkey was Tansu Ciller. During her tenure she actually set foot in the Foreign Ministry on less than a dozen occasions, five of which were visits of 10 to 15 minutes in duration. Throughout this period there were at least three different foreign policies discernible in Turkey:

- That emanating from the foreign ministry, the architect of which was Undersecretary Onur Öymen, a professional diplomat, who in the eyes of many observers was viewed as preoccupied with walking a narrow line between the NSC and the military on one side, and the government which he served on the other—i.e., as having done little to advance the views of the Ministry of Foreign Affairs;

- That espoused by the prime ministry, the policies followed by Necmettin Erbakan, which were typified by a distancing from Turkey's traditional Western allies and a number of attempts to move Turkey more firmly into the Islamic camp of nations. A key architect of this policy was an Erbakan minister of state, one Abdullah Gül;

- Third, and most interesting, the movement by the TGS into the foreign policy arena. Unhappy over Erbakan's overtures to the Islamic world and Ciller's inattention, the TGS actually developed a kind of shadow foreign ministry of its own. Composed of "desks" for each of Turkey's major partners and regional areas of concern, its most notable achievement was the formation of a new policy of strategic cooperation with Israel, a move which clearly had neither the support of Erbakan or Ciller. This effort was orchestrated by the deputy chief of staff, General Cevik Bir, and carried out by the TGS's WWG.

With the advent of the new Yilmaz coalition government this past July, there are important changes discernible in the above formulation. First and foremost, there is now a minister of foreign affairs in fact as well as in name. Ismail Cem, a highly regarded Turkish intellectual (by training a historian, author of several books, former director general of Turkish State Television, long time parliamentarian, former minister of culture, etc.), promises to be a hands-on minister, who immediately upon assuming the portfolio vacated by Ciller sent a clear signal to the Ministry of Foreign Affairs that the days of an absentee minister were over (in his first day as minister he visited each of the sections of the ministry and introduced himself to their staffs). His problems will certainly not stem from any failings of his own. They may however derive from the fact that he has too many people looking over his shoulder. Specifically, Deputy Prime Minister Bülent Ecevit, who fancies himself a foreign policy expert (and who, while Chairman of Ismail Cem's party, is rumored to have had Cem imposed upon him by President Demirel), and Sükrü Gürel, the Minister of State, whose portfolio includes relations with the breakaway Turkish state in Northern Cyprus. In short, Cem is faced with a number of would-be cooks in his kitchen, each of whom may well spoil the broth.

In addition, the role of the TGS's WWG is far from clear. Will it give up its recent attempts at policy formulation and allow the Yilmaz government full freedom of action in foreign and domestic policy? This may be difficult given the fact that in the recent round of promotions/retirements, the key players in the creation of the WWG have retained their positions: İsmail Karadayi, chief of staff, and Çevik Bir, deputy chief of staff.

In the summer of 1997 I had the opportunity to meet with a number of those individuals directly concerned with the formulation and implementation of Turkish foreign policy objectives. They included high-ranking representatives of what I have defined as each of the groups presently involved in shaping the country's policy (the prime ministry, foreign ministry and Turkish General Staff). The following breakdown of items covered in these discussions is presented randomly with no attempt at prioritization. To the extent possible, it reflects a consensus of the views regarding what Turkey's leaders see as some of their major foreign policy complaints, concerns, and problems.

As noted at the outset of this paper, my objective is to communicate these concerns as they were expressed in an attempt to present one side of the equation. In so doing, it is not my intent to serve as anything more than a devil's advocate. To the extent this effort is successful it is designed to provide a framework for further discussion, in the course of which a critique of many of these views will be outlined.

1. Relations with Western Europe are a major concern, in particular the necessity of dealing with the EU's refusal to even set a timetable for Turkey's ultimate integration into the Union while, at the same time, moving forward with a timetable for the integration of the Republic of Cyprus, minus its breakaway Turkish population in the North.

From a Turkish wish perspective there is a hope that the United States will continue pressuring our Western European allies so that Turkey will ultimately configure in whatever plans they have for the future of the European Union. Rejection of Turkey by Europe (in their eyes) will have the effect of: (1) strengthening those forces (Islamic) who argue that Turkey is not Western and that its true place is in the Islamic East, and (2) of proving to the rest of the world that the EU is in fact a Christian club, i.e., of laying the groundwork for an ultimate clash of civilizations as predicted by Huntington. Stated differently, they argue that if Turkey, after 70-plus years of Westernization and 50 years of democratic experience, is unable to fulfill its goal of becoming a full member of the Western world, the message to the rest of the non-Christian world will be clear: Don't bother trying.

Likewise, they state clearly that if the European Union proceeds with plans for the acceptance of the Cypriot Republic into the EU, it means that Turkey will be forced to move toward full economic and ultimate political integration with the Turkish Republic of Northern Cyprus. To both reject any progress in relations with Turkey and move toward integration of Cyprus is a blow which no Western-oriented Turkish government will be able to absorb without responding.

While acknowledging on one level the role played by European concerns over Turkey's less-than-shining human rights record, there is a strong belief that were these problems to disappear overnight it would have no real impact on European attitudes. A new excuse would be proffered for blackballing Turkey from membership in what is at heart a Christian club.

2. Another problem stems from Turkey's growing awareness that the Customs Union they signed with the EU (at Ciller's insistence), has few positive advantages and a large number of disadvantages. There is mounting pressure from the Turkish business community for a reevaluation of this agreement.

Here Turkey hopes that what will almost certainly be an attempt to renegotiate the Customs Union with the EU will not be viewed as a signal that Turkey is pulling back from its longtime goal of full membership in that body—rather, that we accept their view that the Customs Union has failed to either deliver on its promises or smooth the road for Turkey's eventual membership in the EU.

One potential problem here (which Turkish leaders readily acknowledge) is that the United States exerted (at Turkey's insistence) no small degree of pressure on its European allies to get them to accept the Customs Union in the first place. The fact that Ciller's eagerness for acceptance of the Customs Union made her accept less than ideal conditions necessitates a reevaluation which they hope will not be interpreted as ingratitude by Washington.

3. There is a great deal of concern over the issue of bilateral relations with Germany: in particular the variety of problems raised by the presence of two-million-plus Turkish workers in that country and a belief

that German attitudes towards Turkey's EU membership are in reality shaped by these considerations.

Here, Turkey clearly hopes for U.S. assistance in encouraging Germany to separate the bilateral issues on its agenda with Turkey from the question of Turkish EU membership. At present, Germany's shortsighted policy seems to equate the two.

4. A major concern for Turkey's new government is the Cyprus issue: in particular how to handle the increased pressure from Washington for reaching a resolution on this long-festering problem.

Turkey will seek to link a renewed U.S./Holbrooke initiative on Cyprus to the larger question of the EU stance on Turkish and Cypriot membership, respectively. Its position is complicated by the fact that there is no unified Turkish position on terms for a Cyprus resolution. All parties in Turkey seem to feel that a bizonal, bicommunal solution is the minimum which is acceptable. The problems will stem from the differences in the Greek and Turkish definitions of the terms "bizonal" and "bicommunal." If the United States truly buys into the Turkish formula and can sell it to the Greeks, the Holbrooke initiative is promising. Given the variety of voices involved in formulating Turkish foreign policy it does not seem likely that there will be much movement on the Turkish position.

5. Particularly in the foreign ministry there is optimism about the possibility of real progress on resolving bi-lateral issues with its NATO ally Greece, i.e., the Aegean dispute, the Kardak/Imia issue, etc.

Both Greece and Turkey seem to have learned a lesson from the Kardak/Imia crisis. Seemingly, it was the near disaster which may well have helped provide the goodwill which, with a lot of U.S. assistance, led to the Madrid Agreement earlier this summer. The delinkage of bilateral Greco-Turkish problems from the Cyprus issue was obviously an important step, and one would hope that there is a continuing role for the United States in this area. Turkey seems willing to have the United States continue playing the role of middleman in such bilateral issues with Greece, despite a widespread belief that ultimately all U.S.

policy vis-à-vis Greece and Turkey is unduly shaped by the Greek lobby in Washington.

6. The Balkans: in particular the question of Turkey's role in protecting the rights of the descendants of its former Ottoman Muslim populations therein.

While Turkey may (for negotiating purposes) overemphasize the size and importance of its Balkan/Bosnian lobby, i.e., with exaggerated claims of five-plus-million Bosnian Turks in Turkey, the fact of the matter is that a significant percentage of the elite in Turkey do trace their roots to that part of the world. They do relate to the mistreatment of their coreligionists in Bosnia and elsewhere, and they do put pressure on Ankara on their behalf. Consequently, the Balkans are a sensitive issue in Turkish policy and there is an awareness of, and gratitude for, the care with which the United States has taken these concerns into account when deriving its own policy objectives in the region.

7. There may well be a renewed debate on the question of whether or not continued, indeed increased, political, military, and economic cooperation with Israel is in Turkey's interests in light of the universal condemnation it has generated in the Arab world.

By throwing in its lot with Israel on issues of expanding military cooperation, at the very time the Israeli/Palestinian peace process had slowed to a near halt, Turkey was sending a very clear signal to the United States: that this policy, derived from the military's foreign policy efforts rather than from any desire on the part of the Refah government, is also important. Its implementation may thus be interpreted as a rejection of Erbakan's attempts to forge closer ties with his Islamic neighbors, as well as a reinforcement of Turkey's traditional ties to the United States. Regionally Turkey has paid a heavy price for this policy. All factions in the Arab Middle East have condemned the new strategic cooperation policy, and this has had the effect of further isolating Turkey from her Muslim neighbors. While the Turkish military is fully aware of the advantages of this policy (to name a few, access to Israeli technology; cooperation in counterterrorism; training with the superior Israeli Air Force), it seemingly is awaiting some tangible signs of pleasure from Washington for what it also views as a significant contribution to U.S policy objectives in the region.

8. There is growing concern in Turkey over continued Syrian, Iraqi, and Iranian support for the activities of the Kurdish separatist/terrorist PKK groups operating against Turkey from their soils.

While the United States continues to make significant contributions to Turkey's ongoing struggle against the PKK separatist/terrorist insurgency operating out of Syria, Iraq, and Iran, we are seen (in keeping with our overriding concern with the peace process) as likewise sending some rather conflicting signals in the region. When a U.S. secretary of state visits Damascus (the leading supporter of terrorism directed against Turkey) on 20-plus occasions without ever stopping in Ankara, Turkish policymakers clearly wonder as to our priorities. In their view sooner or later we must face the choice of deciding whether attempts to turn Syria into a legitimate member of the family of nations are based on reality or on wishful thinking.

9. There is no unanimity of views on the continued basing in Turkey of "Operation Provide Comfort" (Northern Watch), for the Kurds of northern Iraq. This confusion stems from what is seen in Ankara as the absence of a clear overall U.S. policy on the ultimate future of Iraq (aside from our insistence on maintaining the economic blockade of that country). The blockade against trade with Iraq is viewed in Turkey as a factor in the continued high unemployment in Turkey's Kurdish southeast, and thereby is seen as contributing to the kind of unrest which benefits the PKK.

What is seen as the U.S. policy of: (1) waiting for Saddam Hussein to die, and/or (2) praying that our economic blockade will lead to his ultimate overthrow, is no policy at all when viewed from Ankara. It is seen (rightly or wrongly) as hurting Turkey as much as it hurts Saddam, and this will become an increasing irritant in U.S.-Turkish relations until (and unless) Washington makes its ultimate goals vis-à-vis the Iraqi regime and its Kurdish population clear. There is a great deal of suspicion in Turkish policy circles emanating from this lack of long-term policy, in particular, mistrust over whether or not our ultimate goals in the region will include the creation of an independent Kurdish state in Northern Iraq. Turkish policy objectives (contrary to our own) are based upon a belief that they can deal successfully with Saddam Hussein, and that the Northern Iraqi factions should be pushed into dealing directly with Baghdad.

10. The present government seems deeply concerned over the financial support for fundamentalist Islamic activity in Turkey that is emanating from a variety of regional states: Iran, Saudi Arabia, Sudan, Libya, etc.

Both the Turkish General Staff and the present Yilmaz government seem intent on cracking down on the flow of Islamic fundamentalist money into Turkey—money they see as financing not only the political activity of Refah, but also as providing the infrastructure for numerous other antisecular movements in Turkey. Given the current ease with which questionable money of all colors is helping to fuel the Turkish economy, ironically, it may be a desire to halt the flow of such support for Islamic fundamentalist activity which ultimately forces the government to tighten its policies concerning the flow of all "black money" in and out of Turkey.

11. A major policy concern is Turkish interest in the movement of Caucasus oil and in particular Turkey's role in the pipelines proposed for transporting this resource to the West.

Turkey's efforts to have one or more of the pipelines designed to carry Caspian oil to the west pass through her territory have been largely frustrated by a variety of factors: traditional Russian enmity, the unresolved Azeri-Armenian dispute over the Nagorno-Karabagh enclave, and the heretofore unwillingness of the United States to see Iran as a player in the transport of this resource. Despite these serious drawbacks, Turkey (with the support of Washington) continues to press for pipelines. She does so for the purpose of ensuring her own access to this resource, gaining income from its transshipment over Turkish territory, and limiting the potential danger to its major metropolitan center, Istanbul, should the preferred route of shipment be via giant tankers moving from the Black Sea through the Bosphorus.

12. The still unresolved question of what Turkey's ultimate role in the future of its ethnic cousins the Central Asian Turkic republics and the Caucasus Azerbaijani Republic, continues to be a concern.

Here, despite the initial Özalian-Bushian desire to create a new role for Turkey in the wake of the collapse of the Soviet Union, one which envisioned Turkey (with its supposed links to the Turkic Republics) as the natural corridor for the Western entrée into the region, present-day reality has set in. Both Turkey and the Central Asian republics realize the limitations of their cooperation—limitations imposed by Turkey's inability to make the kind of substantial infrastructural investments needed by the republics, by Russia's desire not to see too strong a Turkish presence in its backyard, and by the fact that the cousins are in fact very distant one from another. However, increased ties in communication, education, and investment all mean that this region will remain important in Turkey's foreign policy concerns. Here, the role expected of the United States may well be one of tempering Russian objections to a Turkish involvement in the region. This stems from a Turkish perception that we are mortgaging their role/involvement as a result of our overriding concern with Russian sensitivities and the survival of Boris Yeltsin.

CONCLUSION

This list serves to illustrate the fact that Turkey does indeed occupy a strategic position in one of the potentially most explosive regions of the world. Its position is complicated by the fact that almost all of its neighbors were at one time or another (for periods ranging from 100 to 500 years) provinces of the Ottoman Empire. As such, their own nationalisms are built to no small extent upon a combination of fear and hatred of the Turks. Any sign of increasing Turkish economic or political strength in the region revives their traditional enmities and this Turcophobia is strong enough to unite Greece, Bulgaria, Romania, Russia, Armenia, Iran, Iraq, and Syria (and most of the rest of the Islamic Middle East) when it comes to undermining any increased regional role for Turkey. This is a fact all too often overlooked by Turkish and U.S. policymakers. While geography dictates an important strategic role for Turkey, history just as strongly ensures that none of her neighbors want to see a strong Turkey.

It is with this rather important caveat in mind that we must approach the question of critical strategic choices in U.S. policy toward Turkey. These are some of what Turkey's political leaders view as their major foreign policy concerns/complaints/problems. The extent to which they mesh (or conflict) with our own policy goals in the region is something which we must determine.

Obviously we are not in a position to meet all of Turkey's expectations, many of which are highly unrealistic, but there must be some give and take. For example, Turks will have to learn to lessen their unrealistic expectations about the extent of American ability to influence our European allies. We in turn, might be well advised to pay more attention to Turkey when it comes to dealing with the likes of Saddam Hussein.

Finally, we have a responsibility to communicate to Turkey's leaders the fact that their *weltanschauung* is not one which we, or anyone else, is likely to fully share. Their all-consuming absorption with maintaining their version of secularism may well need tempering on the eve of the 21st century. In the same way, the Turkish tendency to equate democracy with free elections, often at the expense of paying inadequate attention to human rights, is one which needs modifying, as does the widespread belief that anything which fails to accept the Turkish *weltanschauung* is part of a larger conspiracy on the part of her many foes. In short, our empathy with Turkish goals should not be open-ended. It should be balanced by a desire to ensure that the only Muslim democracy continues to develop in a manner which will indeed make her a model for the rest of the Islamic world.

MEMORANDUM FOR THE PRESIDENT

From: Your Staff
Subject: Summary of Discussion on America and Turkey

This is our summary. It may not necessarily reflect everyone's views, and some may disagree with the conclusions.

1. American leaders should give much more attention to Turkey. Turkey's location at the nexus of Europe, Central Asia, and the Middle East gives tired adjectives like *geopolitical* real meaning, as does the Turkish model of secular governance and pro-American policies. Turkey is also important as a Muslim country that wants engagement with the West, and with Israel.

2. Though participants were uncertain about whether Turkey could contribute significantly to U.S. policy objectives in the Balkans, Ukraine, Central Asia, or the Middle East, all agreed that civil strife or a dramatic change in Turkey's political coloration and orientation could have serious consequences in both Europe and Asia. Extremist political parties have already more than tripled their electoral strength in less than a decade. The Turkish military's "soft coup" earlier this year will not reduce the appeal of such parties to increasingly impoverished and restless voters.

3. Participants favored much more U.S. engagement with and support for Turkey's government, even though the Islamic Refah party has been outlawed. The United States should try to help the new coalition government to succeed, especially with a view toward the parliamentary elections in 1998.

4. Agreement on specifics was more elusive. Some participants felt the necessary implication of more engagement was to organize, take on, and win a major battle with Congress to allow freer sales of arms of Turkey, making this the occasion for raising the public profile of U.S.-Turkish relations and educating American leaders about Turkey's importance. The case was analogized to the 1981 struggle over AWACS sales to Saudi Arabia. Other participants thought that Turkey

was not so interested in buying arms from the United States. Still others were far from eager to join a high-stakes political campaign to support arms sales to Turkey. All acknowledged that the United States will be pressing Turkey to join an American-mediated effort to resolve the Cyprus conflict, though expectations were very modest.

5. Prospects for Turkey are especially ominous unless the Turkish economy can keep up with or outpace Turkey's growing population. Some thought the United States could consider a new policy to aid Turkish economic development, including (1) high-level involvement from the economic agencies of the government, and (2) allowing movement of Iraqi oil through the Turkish pipeline. Others think there is no need for American help, that if Turkey adopts appropriate economic policies the desired private capital will flow in. There were also mixed views about a suggestion for multilateral, conditional assistance along the lines of other IMF efforts in Eastern Europe, Mexico, and East Asia.

6. In relations with Europe, Turkey faces a crisis. Turkish membership in the European Union seems unattainable. The secular Turkish elite has staked much, politically and culturally, on such admission. The European Union is now on course to make a grave problem worse, explosively worse, by preparing to offer the sought-after full accession into the EU to the Greek Cypriot state.

7. Even if the immediate crisis of Cypriot EU accession is headed off, the basic rejection of Turkey will remain, and will rankle. The United States, working closely with interested European countries such as Germany, could concentrate a good deal of effort to find a reassuring arrangement under which Turkey can join Europe, including membership in the European Economic Area (like Norway) and a special status at the European Union's governing bodies in Brussels and Strasbourg.

Questions: How dangerous are the extremists? What are the aims of the Islamic Refah party, or its successor party (or parties)? How should the United States deal with this party?